Ken Connor has been a real stalwart  standing up for the dignity of human li lies regardless of the obstacles. In this b the principles for Christian engagement in the public square and challenge believers to live up to their principles of social justice and good stewardship when determining their political responsibilities. A much-needed book.

—Sam Brownback, *United States Senator*, Kansas

In *Sinful Silence*, Ken Connor and John Revell explore the responsibilities of Christians in a civil society, and make a strong case for renewed faith and accountability among us all. Their work reminds us that we each have a role in government, and encourages us to honor that commitment in our actions every day.

—Jeb Bush, *Governor,* Florida

For years I have appealed to Southern Baptists to join me in earnestly praying for revival to sweep our land. Yet I believe one serious obstacle to revival is our collective failure to obey the Lord's command to act as "salt" and "light," particularly in the area of civil government. I strongly urge you to examine and apply the biblical principles in this book, principles that call us to reflect God and His priorities, even in the civil arena.

—Morris H. Chapman, *President*, SBC Executive Committee

A wonderfully readable, convicting book, challenging Christians to be, as Augustine put it, the best of citizens. This will be a useful guide for Christians to engage the culture faithfully and thoughtfully; it's the kind of equipping the Church desperately needs.

—Charles Colson, *Founder and Past President*,
Prison Fellowship Ministries

Ken Connor and John Revell have produced a very relevant and desperately needed new book entitled: *Sinful Silence: When Christians Neglect Their Civic Duty*. The book shares in a most engaging fashion the need for Christians to be active in every phase of our culture. This is a "must read" for every Christian who does not wish to see our nation sink any further into the mire of godlessness.

—D. James Kennedy, *Pastor,* Coral Ridge Presbyterian Church,
Fort Lauderdale, Florida; *Founder of "Evangelism Explosion"*

From the pen of Ken Connor and John Revell comes a particularly timely and insightful work that looks to God's perspective on ancient Israel's fascination with her neighbors coupled with critical New Testament teachings on Christians' obligation to engage the culture. *Sinful Silence* pulls no punches: Christians bear liability for the moral values promoted by their government. God expects Christians to be involved in their nation's civic affairs and He calls them to make election year decisions according to their understanding of His values.

—Richard Land, *President,*
SBC Ethics & Religious Liberty Commission

Ken Connor and John Revell have written an engaging and compelling book about the obligations of Christian citizenship. Their work provides the evidence for Daniel Webster's observation: "Whatever makes men good Christians makes them good citizens."

—Mel Martinez, *Former U.S. Secretary for Housing and Urban Development*

Our civilization stands not only at a critical moment of decision—it stands on the brink of crisis. The intellectual, ideological, moral, and political fault lines of our contemporary conflict all point to a fundamental spiritual problem. Far too many Christians fail to bring Christian conviction into the public square and fail to speak out when silence is indeed sinful. Ken Connor and John Revell have issued a manifesto that should awaken the church, embarrass the silent, and embolden a new generation of Christians to courageous truth telling. Every Christian should read this book.

—R. Albert Mohler, Jr., *President,*
The Southern Baptist Theological Seminary, Louisville, Kentucky

At first sight of the impending release of *Sinful Silence* I made a note, "Get this book now!" Both authors are personal acquaintances and dynamic Christians with whom I have had the privilege to serve the Lord. Outside of the fact that Christians neglect their obligations to do personal soul winning, nothing needs more concern than our civic duty before God. "Get this book now!"

—Bobby H. Welch, *Pastor,* First Baptist Church, Daytona Beach, Florida; *Originator* of the "FAITH" evangelism strategy

SINFUL SILENCE

WHEN CHRISTIANS NEGLECT THEIR CIVIC DUTY

Ken Connor and John Revell

ginosko
PUBLISHING
"...to know and love God
and His Word."

Cover design by John Revell
Cover art by Andy Beachum

Dedication

This book is dedicated first and foremost to the Glory of God,

And to our children:

Ken and Amy's—Kathryn, Elizabeth, Caleb, and Joshua

and

John and Debbie's—Micah and Philip.

Our prayer is that you will be able
to raise your children in a just and free society.

Table of Contents

Introduction

Many Christians in the U. S. appear to have a poor understanding of what God expects regarding their participation in the civil process—and that's understandable because they have been told so many things. Some have concluded that voting and civil involvement is optional. Others seem to view involvement as a necessary evil at best, and "dirty" or wordly at worst. A few years ago, one popular book even suggested that Christian political organizations are misguided and perhaps even harmful.

On the other hand some seem to think that supporting and participating in a political organization or party meets most of God's expectations. Some even act as if God has given His unique endorsement to their particular candidate or party.

The tragedy is that too many of us have formed our opinions and carved out our convictions without looking to God for *His* direction—and where do we find that direction but in His Word?

Sinful Silence presents biblical principles that will remove any doubt as to God's heart on the issue of civil involvement. We have attempted to present a compelling case from the writings of the mighty prophet Isaiah—a case that will likely alarm you—but a case that will hopefully draw you into a closer walk with God. And, after reading this book, we pray you will be far more motivated to participate in the civil processes of our great nation.

You need to understand that the message in this book is likely to offend and convict members of both major political parties. The goal of this book, however, is not the success of any political organization, party, or candidate, but rather the application of salt and light in a dark and decaying society. We encourage you to read it carefully and prayerfully—if you do, and if you follow through, and if others do the same, the resulting spiritual impact upon our nation could be dramatic and profound.

—Ken Connor and John Revell, June, 2004

Chapter 1

SHARED RESPONSIBILITY, SHARED GUILT

The shades on the two east windows were open, and beams of morning sunlight flooded the Executive Office—yet his mood was dark. An overstuffed chair held his weary body while a handcrafted desk of Philippine mahogany supported his arms and heavy head. Matching mahogany paneling surrounded the room, covering the lower half of the walls and reaching down to a floor blanketed with deep pile carpet. The drapes adorning each of the three windows cost the state more than its average employee's annual salary. Portraits of past statesmen who had gone on to serve inside the nation's Beltway rested against heavily flocked wallpaper, keeping silent and sympathetic sentry over an office where power and money were brokered daily.

These types of surroundings have fed the dreams of most young, aspiring politicians. Indeed, many have fantasized about sitting in this very office, in this very chair, at this very desk. However, the rocky road to his office was littered with the broken lives and battered families of those who faltered on their dream-driven quest to become governor of this great state. Few, if any of them, recognized that after reaching the office, a mere thread separated the dream from a nightmare. This morning that thread had broken once again, and the

Honorable Peter James (P.J.) Bates was fighting to survive yet another nightmare.

Throwing his head and weight back into the chair, he lifted his gaze to the ceiling, focusing on nothing in particular. "Is it possible? How could it be? How could it happen again?" he asked the empty room. According to the morning edition of the *Tribune*, which lay on the desk before him, another of his executive level appointees had been indicted.

The person and position were different, but the horror had become all too familiar. This time it was John Billings, the Secretary of Housing, and the charge was racketeering. Nancy Jenkins, the senior investigative reporter for the capital's daily paper, reported on evidence that Billings had been funneling state-funded, low-income housing contracts to his old construction company through a minority-controlled shell corporation.

"How could Billings have come this far and still be so stupid? There are ways to walk in 'gray' areas safely. If he hasn't learned that by now, he deserves what he gets. But why should I have to suffer for his ineptness? Why should my reelection be jeopardized by some fool who didn't listen to his dime-store attorney?"

Three years earlier Bates had trusted his campaign aides to provide names for appointments. They had done a stellar job in managing his campaign, and their network of resources was enviable. Certainly they could provide the names of qualified individuals for these posts while he concentrated on the early draft of the budget. Unfortunately, their management skills had fallen short in the area of background checks. Now, for the fourth time in three years, Bates had to focus his attention on separating himself and his position from the accused.

Lowering his head somewhat, he propped his right elbow on the arm of his chair and lifted a pencil to his mouth, placing the eraser on his lower lip (his staff had seen the habit countless times and would have known that it signaled a forthcoming strategy). Could Tommy Johnson, his press secretary—and perhaps his most valued asset—pull it off again?

When asked about the frequency of indictments in this administration, could he go back to the good folks of this state and remind them that, "Gov. Bates could not and should not be held responsible for the actions of another. No innocent party should bear the burden of another's guilt, and no fair-minded person would impose that burden on our governor. After all, Governor Peter Bates has repeatedly, emphatically, and publicly decried this kind of behavior, especially from a steward of the public's trust.

"Mr. Billings is innocent until proven guilty, of course, and Gov. Bates has absolute confidence that our justice system will be both effective and efficient. Besides, some members of the opposition party may have exaggerated the claims that led to the investigation in the first place. But, regardless of the outcome, the citizens of this great state must remember that this is not about the governor; it's about John Billings."

Peter Bates leaned forward and pushed the intercom. "Liz, get ahold of Tommy and send him over right away." He leaned back in his chair and glanced over at the eastern windows. Briefly irritated, he wondered if there were any way to get more light into the room.

When the reporters finally press Tommy Johnson, should the good people of this fictitious state accept his response? Is it accurate to suggest that Gov. Bates is not responsible in any way for the actions and failures of his appointees? While sympathetic politicians might hope so, in reality we know that Gov. Bates should be held accountable—to a degree—for the character and actions of his appointee, John Billings.

When the people choose a leader who is expected to make appointments, the activity of those appointees reflects upon the elected leader. If an appointee makes wise decisions that profit the people, it's proper for the appointing leader to share the credit. By the same token, when an appointee fails in his or her responsibilities, or when that appointee is involved in unethical and immoral activities, the people are justified in holding the elected leader accountable. In this situation, the one responsible for the appointment shares a level of guilt.

Few of us would have a problem with this principle. In fact, in the example of P.J. Bates, we might throw hearty support behind statements such as: "That's why they get paid the big bucks;" "If you can't take the heat, get out of the kitchen;" and the ever popular "Throw the rascals out!" We understand the responsibility placed on an elected leader to make wise decisions and appointments. We also understand that when an elected leader's appointee makes poor decisions or acts unethically, the leader is accountable and answerable to the ones who placed him or her in office.

But does this link between responsibility and accountability also apply on a larger scale to the state or nation that appoints leaders to office? When elected officials make unwise, unethical, and immoral decisions, doesn't that reflect on the citizens who chose them? If a nation shares the responsibility of choosing leadership, and if that nation elects unwise or unethical leaders, isn't it also true that the nation itself shares a level of their guilt and is held accountable for the far-reaching failures of those leaders? If it is true, then to whom are the citizens accountable and before whom do they stand guilty?

These questions may seem strange, for we usually don't think along these lines. The answers may even make us a bit uncomfortable. If the account of Gov. Bates were an isolated event, the question would probably be irrelevant. However, over the last thirty-five years, some reporters have earned their paychecks and secured comfortable retirements by covering a growing number of similar cases.

Sadly, the stories have become so commonplace that they no longer shock us. Watergate stunned the American public and dominated the nation's attention. Today a similar situation may no longer be considered newsworthy. Because of this trend in our nation, perhaps it is time to seriously consider these questions and address the implications of their answers. Do we, the citizens, share accountability for the unbiblical policies and decisions of our leaders? If so, to whom will we answer?

The nation of Judah faced similar questions. When God first established Israel, Judah was part of the larger nation. But when King Solomon died, Israel and Judah divided into two independent nations. During the two hundred years following Judah's birth as an independent nation, she experienced the intense blessings of prosperity followed by the deadly curse of national arrogance, greed, and lust.

Judah's wickedness climaxed when King Ahaz exchanged the nation's religious and moral foundations for political gain (2 Kings 16:1-12). Because of God's special relationship with Judah, He had every right to ask for and expect her allegiance and obedience. When she stubbornly disobeyed Him and ignored His principles in government, God condemned her behavior through the prophets.

The most vocal of these men was the mighty prophet Isaiah. In his writings we encounter God's passion for the nation's civil responsibilities and His justified anger over their neglect. But we also find timeless lessons and principles for civil government—

principles that span the ages and cultural barriers and apply to us and our own government. As we consider a portion of God's message to Judah through Isaiah, we will discover the answer to our first question: Do we as U.S. citizens share accountability for the civil sins of our leaders, and if so, to whom must we render an accounting?

GOD'S WORD

In Isaiah's first chapter the prophet removes any doubt about God's passion regarding national accountability for civil sins. In fact, Isaiah directly linked the people's guilt with the leaders' guilt. In dramatic style he candidly challenges the people of Judah, declaring, *Hear the word of the LORD, you rulers of Sodom; listen to the law of our God, you people of Gomorrah!* (Isa. 1:10). In that one declaration, the people of Judah were struck by the force of God's accusation.

Isaiah's reference to these two ancient cities may not mean much to us today, but to the citizens and leaders of Judah the comparison was dark and ominous. The mention of Sodom and Gomorrah produced vivid images in the minds of God's people, pictures of extreme wickedness and severe judgment. Long before the formation of Judah, God dealt with these cities and destroyed them because of their wickedness. In the Genesis story, we find an account of perversion, debauchery, and judgment that is unequalled in human history.

A Shocking Sin

When Isaiah equated the leaders and people of Judah with Sodom and Gomorrah, they should have been shocked into understanding God's fury over their sin. But what had they done that had made Him so angry? The men of Judah had not attempted to gang rape innocent young men—what would have justified such a radical comparison?

What behavior could be so horrid that God would compare His people to such an extreme level of wickedness?

Isaiah revealed their wickedness in 1:17, where he declared that the nation had failed to: *Seek justice, encourage the oppressed. Defend the cause of the fatherless, plead the case of the widow.* Isaiah continued the indictment in verse 23, where he proclaimed: *Your rulers are rebels, companions of thieves; they all love bribes and chase after gifts. They do not defend the cause of the fatherless; the widow's case does not come before them.*

This alarming indictment was because of Judah's *civil* sin. The national leadership had failed miserably in three key areas of civil responsibility: justice, deliverance from oppression, and protection for the helpless. God explicitly identified this failure in verse 16 as "evil" and equated these civil sins with the depravity of Sodom and Gomorrah.

Civil sins weren't the only ones that concerned Isaiah, however. Later in his writings he identified additional national and individual rebellion that warranted God's severe judgment. We will consider some of those sins later, but in this portion of Isaiah's message, based on the immediate context, this *specific* equation with Sodom and Gomorrah is *directly* linked to civil corruption and failure.

An Ominous Association

But why would a fair and just God include the general population of Judah in this indictment? These failures came from Judah's national leadership, not the average person on the street. In other portions of Isaiah's book, we find examples of individual sins that would justify such a rebuke, but the context of this passage directly connects the citizens with the sins of their leaders. Wouldn't it be unfair to punish all of the people of Judah for the civil sins and failures of the government?

If the people had been given no say in the choice and appointment of their leaders, these questions might have substance. However, when we look closely at Judah's broader history, we find that God had indeed given the people a key role in deciding their leadership. When Moses led the Jewish people out of Egypt to Mt. Sinai, he gave very clear and specific guidelines for the appointment of civil leaders.

In Deuteronomy 16: 18-20, Moses told the people God's plan for determining local leadership. He commanded them to: *Appoint judges and officials for each of your tribes in every town the LORD your God is giving you, and they shall judge the people fairly. Do not pervert justice or show partiality. Do not accept a bribe ... Follow justice and justice alone, so that you may live and possess the land the LORD your God is giving you.* He carefully instructed them that when they settled in the new land, they were to appoint for themselves civil leaders in each local area. These leaders were expected to uphold justice, to be completely impartial, and to absolutely avoid the temptation of bribes. This system of appointment should not be equated with modern democratic elections. Yet, as Kalland points out, God placed the responsibility for these civil expectations squarely on the shoulders of the people.[1] There is no evidence that God had canceled or rescinded this design for the Jewish nation during Isaiah's time.

The *people* were responsible for selecting qualified individuals who would then be approved and installed by the religious leaders. In addition, Moses' instruction was not addressed primarily to the future leaders but to all of the *people* of the land. In this command, he placed the responsibility for justice and civil morality upon the shoulders of the people, who were to fulfill the command through the appointment of qualified leaders.

Further, Moses said in 17:14-15: *When you enter the land the LORD your God is giving you and have taken possession of it and settled in it, and you say, "Let us set a king over us like all the nations around us," be sure to appoint over you the king the LORD your God chooses.* Here he indicated that God would ultimately choose the king. Yet the instruction placed the burden of *confirming* future kings upon the people![2]

These glimpses of Judah's earliest foundations demonstrate us that while the people didn't have *absolute* authority in the selection of leaders, they played a vital role in a leader's appointment. God's design gave His people a high level of responsibility in the appointment of local leaders and the confirmation of kings. For this reason, they had an equally high level of accountability for those leaders' actions.

According to Deuteronomy 16:20, if the people appointed qualified, moral leaders, the nation would share in the richest of God's blessings. On the other hand, the presence of unjust and greedy leaders would clearly show that the people as a whole had failed in their responsibility. While God promised rich blessings for those who obeyed, He also promised harsh punishment for those who disobeyed (Deut. 28:1-68). Because the people shared the responsibility in appointing leaders, they also were positioned to share the guilt and consequences of failed leadership.

When we return to Isaiah's scathing rebuke, we can now see that he was directly confronting this joint failure. According to verses 17 and 23, the leaders were unjust in their rulings, partial to the rich, and used their positions for financial gain. Their activities blatantly violated God's requirements for civil leadership. Therefore, because the people had been given a voice and because the leaders were civil and moral failures, the people shared the guilt of their leaders.[3]

When God indicted the civil leaders of Judah for their failures, the people who appointed these leaders (or *allowed* them by their silence to be appointed) were jointly accountable to God and stood equally guilty before Him.

THE U.S. IN COMPARISON

In light of Judah's history, the logical question is, "What (if any) implications does Judah, 730 B.C., have for the United States, A.D. 2004?"

God held the people of Judah accountable for their leaders' sins, in part because He gave them a significant responsibility in selecting their leaders. But if we consider our own form of civil government in light of Judah's, we may find that the citizens of the United States are subject to an even stronger judgment.

Our Structure

The citizens of the United States elect the president, vice-president, and all the members of Congress. When we place these leaders in office, we expect the executive and legislative branches to set civil and social policies for our nation. Also, these leaders take a stand on a range of moral issues such as abortion, same-sex "marriage," euthanasia, assisted suicide, and so forth. Whether we like it or not, the decisions of these leaders directly impact the moral direction of our nation. Therefore, the people's vote (or failure to vote) ultimately determines our nation's civil, social, and moral direction.

Furthermore, the president appoints each member of the federal judiciary, who is then confirmed by the Senate. These judges are expected to interpret laws and make legal decisions that affect the entire nation. Therefore, the citizen's role in each election also sets the tone for the judicial branch of government. Each person's voice (or silence) directly impacts every level of government.

The people's role in selecting their leaders is neither an accident nor the product of societal evolution. Over two hundred years ago the framers of our constitution set out to design a governmental system that would be "of the people, for the people and by the people." As they labored for months, they were driven by recent and bitter memories of the Revolutionary War. Each bore vivid mental images of friends and family members who sacrificed dearly to secure freedom from tyranny. Therefore, the constitutional authors sought to establish a system that would provide the citizens a voice in government and protect this newborn nation from future threats of tyranny.

These governmental architects rejected the model of a pure "democracy," in which each individual has an actual vote on virtually every issue in the government. Instead, they opted for a "constitutional republic," in which the government would operate through elected representatives. Under this model, each citizen would be represented in government by individuals specifically chosen and placed into office by the citizens. Our founding fathers deliberately placed the responsibility of appointing leaders upon the shoulders of each citizen. Thus, a new government was born.

Because the American system is a representative form of government, there is an obvious relationship between an elected leader's actions and the citizens who elected the leader. While the people themselves do not govern directly (as is the case in a democracy), their representatives are the primary decision makers in matters of public policy.

In legal terms, our elected leaders are "agents" of the American people who act as "principals." Furthermore, it is well established in law that the actions of agents legally bind their principals. A principal is held liable and accountable for the actions of his or her agent, even if the principal were not directly involved in the action. Therefore, we as citizens are liable for the decisions of our elected representative leaders, even if we are not directly involved in their activities.

If we do not agree with the direction of our elected leaders, we are free to replace those leaders through the electoral process. If leadership does not change, it is safe to assume that the leaders' actions accurately reflect the desires and priorities of the majority of the people. If we do not vote to change leaders, we send a message to our leaders—as well as to our nation, to our world, and to God—that we support the views and policies of existing leaders. As a nation, we the citizens have the corporate freedom and responsibility to choose our leaders, so we are corporately responsible for their civil, social, and moral leadership.

This historical review demonstrates that our governmental situation is similar to Judah's in at least one way: The people had a voice in the selection of their leaders. If a leader was irresponsible, unjust, or immoral, the people could only blame themselves for allowing this person to continue in such a role.

Nevertheless, there are some major differences between the two governments that we dare not ignore. First, the Jewish people were functioning as a theocracy under which God gave the people a voice in the selection of their leaders. We, on the other hand, function as a democratic republic where leaders are elected by the citizens to represent the citizens.

Second, the entire nation of Judah was seen as the chosen people of God, and their government was established from the very beginning to reflect that relationship.[4] At best, only *some* of the U.S. population claim to be God's people, and our governmental structure was not designed to show that theocratic relationship. The intent and overall structure of each government is completely different.

Third, there was a legal, covenant relationship between God and His people that *He* initiated (Deut. 29:9-15). This covenant had a direct bearing on their government, and in Isaiah's day that covenant had been broken by the people. While the covenant system strongly influenced the shaping of America's government, it simply can't be said that God initiated the same type of relationship between Himself and our government that He did with the nation of Judah.

When we consider all of these contrasts (and there are more), we find that there are very few similarities between the two governments and nations. Since our setting and structure are so different from that of Isaiah's day, is it really fair to link the U.S. so closely with Judah's indictment? One could accurately point out that God had a unique relationship with Judah and that the history of His dealings with Judah's example and experience doesn't necessarily impact the United States. So, does the example of Judah have any true relevance for the United States?

The One True King

If God's passion for government were restricted to His concern for the civil functions of Judah, this link would be unfair. However, the Bible is clear and emphatic throughout on this issue. Beyond His concern for Judah's civil structure and activities, God has specific expectations of, and absolute authority over, *all* governments. In fact, the Scriptures bluntly declare that all governments and civil leaders exist because of God and that He is their ultimate source of authority.[5]

Furthermore, the Bible teaches that God promises and delivers severe judgment upon governments that violate His civil standards. Throughout the Scriptures there are multiple examples of governments that defied God's civil standards and felt His wrath.[6]

23

God's expectations, authority, and judgment of civil governments were not reserved for Judah alone. He has clear expectations of *all* governments; He has absolute authority over *all* governments; and He is in a position to pronounce judgment upon *all* disobedient governments. So, while our situation and structure may differ profoundly from Judah's, the government of the United States of America is still subject to God's expectations, authority, and judgment.

The example of Judah illustrates a principle that has direct bearing on our own civil government: *When the citizens have a voice in the selection and direction of their civil leaders, God holds both the leaders and the citizens accountable for the civil sins of the government.* In Judah we find an example of people who had a voice in selecting their leaders and who were accountable to God for their leaders' actions—the fact that they had a special relationship with God does not invalidate the illustration. Their civil leaders and structure failed God's expectations, and they had to answer to Him for those failures. Judah serves as a powerful and sobering example of God's judgment upon a government in which greedy and unjust leaders were either approved by the people or were allowed into leadership positions through the apathetic silence of the people.

Furthermore, as we have seen, ours is a government "of the people, for the people and by the people." In the U.S., the citizens are responsible for determining who will govern us. In effect, *we* decide who will lead us; therefore, the *citizens* are ultimately responsible for the activities of our elected officials.

Therefore, because of the example of Judah, and because of our own civil structure in the U.S., and in light of God's ultimate authority over all governments, it logically follows that God holds the citizens of the U.S. corporately accountable for the actions of our leaders. Because of our participation as citizens (or our *failure* to participate) in electing leaders to office and holding them accountable while in office, we share corporate responsibility for the actions and decisions of those individuals. It makes sense that when our nation's governmental actions continually and consistently defy God's priorities, He would hold us, the corporate citizenship of the United States, directly accountable.

Finally, those of us in the U.S. who claim to follow God's Word bear a higher level of responsibility than those who do not make such a claim. We may be citizens of God's Kingdom first, but we are still expected to function as responsible citizens in this earthly kingdom. Through the Scriptures we can determine God's expectations of our government. And, as we've already seen, each of us has direct access to the decision-making process in our states and in our nation. We have no excuse! If we are irresponsible in our voting or if we fail to vote, we cannot escape accountability before God. If we don't hold officials accountable (as best we can) after their election, we may indeed share the burden of guilt.

Each one of us has the ability to impact all of society in a positive way through our vote and then through our input to elected officials. When we choose to ignore this process, we reflect the same sin that plagued Judah during Isaiah's time. And as we have seen, God does not stand on the sidelines, a passive spectator in our nation's civil arena. Rather, He is passionate in His expectations of us as citizens who can make a positive difference.

CONCLUSION

Because of God's position over and expectations of our governmental leaders, because our civil structure allows us to choose and direct our leaders, and in light of the example of

Judah's failure in this area, we must face the fact that the citizens of the United States of America share corporate accountability before God for our leaders' civil sins. When our government's policies defy God's Word, it's not merely "their" (the leaders') sin; it is "our" (the nation's) sin.

U.S. citizens have not only a civic duty but also a spiritual responsibility to vote. After voting, we have the same obligation before God to hold elected officials accountable to His standards for government. If as individuals we make an honest effort to elect qualified leaders, and if we are faithful to call our elected leaders to reflect our moral convictions on civil matters, there is no reason to expect God to hold us *individually* accountable. But, when we fail in this responsibility, we not only fail our government, we fail God; and we should not be shocked at the massive national consequences of these failures, consequences that the Christian community may indeed experience because of its corresponding silence at the polls. When Christians neglect their civil duty, they need not expect deliverance from the national consequences to follow.

Over the last thirty years, our states and our nation have provided far too many examples similar to that of Gov. P.J. Bates. In each instance, from Watergate to "Whatever-gate," we've been outraged that our public trust was violated. Those officials who have violated God's standards for civil government will one day answer directly to Him.

However, in each instance we must remember who was responsible for placing these individuals in office. Who allowed them the position and authority to make decisions and appointments that have contributed to our national moral crisis? Who empowered them to bring gradual destruction upon us? *We* are the ones. When we, the citizens, apathetically and haphazardly elect (*or, even worse, allow their election by not voting*) leaders who are personally and politically corrupt, *we* share corporate accountability before God for their civil failures. And one day, along with those leaders, we may be corporately forced to face God's judgment upon our land.

---

1. Earl Kalland, *The Expositor's Bible Commentary, "Deuteronomy,"* vol. 3, (Grand Rapids: Zondervan Publishing House, 1992), 112.

2. John Bright, A *History of Israel, Third Edition,* (Philadelphia: Westminster Press, 1981), 188, 196,198. The implication was that until the people confirmed the king, his position and authority was not yet official. Consider the illustrations of Saul and David. Both had been anointed by Samuel, but neither was official until the people collectively recognized them. Also, because of his cruelty, the people of Israel rejected Rehoboam as their king and God honored that rejection. They confirmed Jeroboam as their king and God honored that confirmation. Both situations had been decreed by God, but He used the peoples' rejection and confirmation to execute His decree. Nevertheless, these demonstrate the people's legal ability to reject an unfit king and install another. All four of these were in keeping with the instruction of Deuteronomy 17:15. Also, see Kalland, Ibid.

3. Consider the fact that Isaiah's address in 1:17 is not directed primarily to the leaders but *jointly* to the people and the leaders. Also, the accusation of verse 23 is directed toward the people, chastising them because their rulers and leaders were corrupt. Isaiah further addressed this connection between the people and the sins of the leaders in 3:13-15; 5:7; 5:14; 5:23, 25. This clearly indicates a shared accountability on the part of the people for the civil sins of their leaders.

4. Deuteronomy 1:16-17; 7:6-9; 10:15; 29:9-15.

5. Consider Psalm 2; Proverbs 8:14-16; Daniel 4:19-37, especially verses 25 and 34; John 19:10,11; Romans 13:1-7; Ephesians1:20-22; Philippians 2:9-11; 1 Timothy 6:13-15; Revelation 1:5; 17:14; 19:16.

6. In Amos 1:3-2:3, God promised His judgment through national destruction to six nations that neighbored Judah and Israel. In four of these indicted nations, the respective kings were specified as guilty. The crimes mentioned in each of these cases were committed by the governments of the nations, and the judgments were directly related to governmental depravity.
   In addition to Amos, the prophesies of Jonah and Nahum were directed toward the kingdom of Assyria. History reveals that their kings and armies were ruthless and brutal in their conquests. Nahum 3:18,19 and Jonah 3:4-9 (especially v. 8) link God's judgment with this cruelty. (for additional passages showing God's judgment on kings and nations, see Ps. 2:10-12; Ezek. chapters 26-32 & 38; 39; Dan. 5:18-30; Rev. 6:15,16; 19:17-21.)

Chapter 2

WASTED WORSHIP

Liz hurried down the sidewalk toward to The Golden Dome Café. An uneasy glance at her watch confirmed that she would be late for her lunch with Barb. For thirteen years, Barbara Stevens and Elizabeth Thompson had celebrated each other's brightest moments and bolstered each other through their darkest hours. With that history, Liz knew that Barb wouldn't be upset, but she didn't like to keep her waiting.

Liz pushed open the door to The Dome (as the locals call it) and saw Barb's smile light up the corner. She rushed over and apologized as she slid into the booth, explaining that Gov. Bates had dictated an urgent, last-minute memo. Barb brushed it off. After six years as the pastor's secretary at the Capital First Baptist Church, she was a seasoned veteran in "urgent, last minute" assignments.

Their waitress, Toni, strolled over with her pad and removed the pencil from behind her right ear to take their order—but only as a formality. Every Thursday for the last three years these two had ordered the same lunch, and she could jot down the order from memory.

Liz started. "I'll have the ham and cheese on rye with lettuce, tomato, and mustard, but no mayo—too much fat, you know. And instead of chips, could I have a small salad with 'lite' dressing? Let's see ... to drink I'll have the diet cola. Also, is the apple pie fresh today? Ooh ... I really shouldn't do this, but for dessert I think I'll have a slice, heated please, with a very small scoop of ice cream."

"I'll have the same," chimed Barb.

As Toni stepped away, Barb leaned over the table and lowered her voice slightly. "I read about John Billings's indictment in the morning paper. How is the governor doing?"

"Not very well," Liz replied. "He's really tense. When things start to get to him, he has a nervous habit of pushing his glasses up on his nose all the time, even when he doesn't need to. Well, he's been pushing those glasses all morning. I really don't think he's going to survive this one. There seems to be a lot of evidence."

"I know," Barb offered. "The article paints an ugly picture, doesn't it? I almost mentioned it this morning for prayer in staff meeting."

"Oh, Barb, you're so thoughtful," Liz responded.

"I said I *almost* mentioned it for prayer," answered Barb. "I didn't, because I thought it might bother Pastor Benson. You know how he is about mixing politics and religion. He has always felt that the church is not the place for political matters, and he's been very deter-mined to keep all government issues outside the church walls.

"Also, there is such a strong mix of both political parties in our church. Pastor avoids any discussion of government or politics because he's afraid it will divide the congregation. He's been very careful not to step on any political toes.

"Besides," she added, "I could see that Pastor Benson was already upset about something this morning. For several weeks he has seemed down for some reason. Well, this morning he opened up to us all and poured out his frustrations at what has happened—or, actually, what has *not* happened—over the last year."

Toni dropped off their order so they stopped briefly to bow their heads and quietly thank the Lord. Then Liz picked up her sandwich and probed further, asking, "Why, what's going on?"

"Well," Barb continued, "this last year was packed full with activities that should have helped our church to grow. All along we've had good Sunday morning services. But this year we also had the fall revival services, a special week of prayer, intense teacher training for Sunday School teachers, and special training in evangelism. The whole staff went to the evangelism conference last year, and they came back all fired up. Pastor Benson feels that since we've built the new sanctuary, we've had all of the ingredients for church growth.

"But, instead of growth, it seems like nothing has changed in the church for a long time. Some folks have made emotional, public decisions to be more committed to the Lord, but most of those people have been making those same decisions for years. A number of people have been baptized, but only a couple of them are still coming.

"What makes it worse," she noted, "is that over the years, the same people seem to be struggling with the same problems. The folks who have had long-term drinking problems are still struggling. Pastor Benson seems to be counseling the same people this year as he was last year. No one seems to change. Besides that, there's all the normal gossip and fighting. And you already know about the affairs and divorces we've had in our church. Pastor feels like it has all been a waste of time. This morning he broke down crying and said that he feels like God doesn't hear our prayers anymore. We were all stunned and didn't know what to say."

"Wow," Liz sighed, "the cloud over this city is bigger than I thought."

THE SPIRITUAL STATE OF THE UNION

Capital First Baptist Church isn't unique, is it? Tragically, many churches across the land can identify with their plight. In fact, there may be a multitude of pastors who can relate directly to Pastor Benson's frustration and despair. Sometimes it just doesn't make sense. The Bible tells us that because of Jesus' sacrificial death for our sin, we can repent and ask forgiveness for our sin. The result is *supposed* to be a changed life, one that has been freed from slavery to sin—a life that is radically different from those who don't follow Him.

We also are taught that the local church is a strategic key in introducing and promoting that change. Consequently, we pour our energy into the exciting task of reaching people with this good news. We teach and train our folks to evangelize. We pray diligently for the Lord to sweep our church, our community, our city, our state, and our nation with a life-changing, spiritual "revival." And we slave feverishly over weekly worship services that will hopefully stir hearts and souls.

But something is missing from the equation. If following Jesus is supposed to result in a changed life, where are all of the shining examples of changed lives? Also, if participation in church worship, programs, and prayer is supposed to help in this change process, we've not made the connection somewhere. There are plenty of folks who claim to follow Jesus but whose lives tell a different story. We have no shortage of worship services across the nation each Sunday morning, but it seems that many people, if not most, leave those services no different than when they entered.

Recent surveys seem to verify this contradiction. According to pollster George Barna, true revival does not appear to be sweeping the land. In his research, he has discovered that there may be pockets of revival in certain portions of our nation, but overall, people's attitudes and priorities do not reflect a significant change.[1]

Yet in 2004, nearly nine out of ten adults claim that their religious faith is very important to them.[2] Also, seven out of ten people believe that God is the all-powerful, all-knowing Creator of the universe who still rules the world today.[3] Forty-three percent of American adults said they attend church in a typical weekend.[4] And, about 78 percent of adults donated money to a non-profit organization or a church in 2000 with the average donor contributing a mean of $649.[5] Finally, 37 percent of those surveyed said that they prayed at least once a day, and 82 percent said that they believe that prayer can change what happens in a person's life.[6]

The majority of our population appears to participate in church and related activities (at least on a limited scale), but there is a critical deficit when we look for a positive spiritual impact upon the land. For some reason, God doesn't seem to be answering our prayers for national revival. William Bennett reports that between 1960 and 1999, the percentage of out-of-wedlock births increased 523 percent, and the number of cohabiting couples increased from 439,000 in 1960 to 4.24 million in 1998—an almost tenfold increase![7] The suicide rate for those between 15 and 24 has tripled over the past twenty-five years,[8] and the divorce rate in 2003 was twice the rate in 1960.[9]

Ironically, from 1970-2000 the Southern Baptist Convention reported that almost 13,000,000 people were converted to faith in Jesus Christ and baptized through their churches.[10] This doesn't even take into consideration all of the conversions reported from other denominations. We have seen professions of faith—but where are the changed lives? Where is the infusion of "salt" and "light" into our society that should logically follow such numbers? Where is the revival in our churches for which we've prayed? In fact, while there may be some small pockets of God's blessing, there is little evidence that God is working through our churches and their activities on a national level.

Why is this so? Is it possible that we have misunderstood the Lord's direction and that we should not expect any change? Perhaps we have our sights set too high and should be more reasonable in our expectations.

Or ... perhaps there is another explanation. Could it be that something is hindering our prayers? Psalm 66:18 teaches that God doesn't listen to our prayers when we "cherish" sin in our hearts. Suppose there is a sin problem that is somehow infecting churches across the entire nation and, in turn, is interfering with our combined prayers for national revival. If this is the case, then what sin could be so widespread and permeate so deeply that it could interfere with prayer on such a large scale?

Consider this option: What if our failure as God's people to recognize and address blatant violations of God's civil standards has somehow hindered our prayer and worship?

Initially this idea may seem far-fetched—but remember that our governmental structure relies upon the citizens to choose and direct their leaders. Also, remember that when we fail to exercise these rights and responsibilities, God holds us accountable for the civil sins of our leaders.

Now, what if the spiritual consequences of our civil silence have gone even deeper? What if God is ignoring prayers for revival and rejecting our widespread worship activities because we have ignored His expectations of our government? What if the majority of prayer and worship in this nation is a massive waste of time because God refuses to receive it?

Think back to Pastor Benson and his dilemma. Is it possible that the spiritual stagnancy in Capital First Baptist is linked to the refusal to address clear moral issues in the civic arena? This notion may seem extreme, but let's return to the example of Judah and see how their civil sins impacted their worship.

GOD'S WORD

In the last chapter we found Isaiah's shocking equation of the people of Judah to the infamous cities of Sodom and Gomorrah. But that was just the start of this prophetic bombshell. In the verses following that initial indictment, Isaiah struck at the very core of Judah's heritage in worship. He further exposed God's passion on the matter, proclaiming:

"The multitude of your sacrifices—what are they to me?" says the Lord. "I have more than enough of burnt offerings, of rams and the fat of fattened animals; I have no pleasure in the blood of bulls and lambs and goats. When you come to appear before me, who has asked this of you, this trampling of my courts? Stop bringing meaningless offerings! Your incense is detestable to me. New Moons, Sabbaths and convocations—I cannot bear your evil assemblies. Your New Moon festivals and your appointed feasts my soul hates. They have become a burden to me; I am weary of bearing them. When you spread out your hands in prayer, I will hide my eyes from you; even if you offer many prayers, I will not listen. Your hands are full of blood;" (Isa. 1:11-15).

In dramatic fashion Isaiah revealed that God had utterly rejected Judah's offerings and sacrifices, completely ignored their assemblies of worship and celebration, and absolutely refused to hear their prayers. These three areas of worship represented the sum total of Judah's entire religious life, and Isaiah informed them that their worship was a complete waste of time because God refused to receive it. This announcement should have been catastrophic for the people of Judah.

Judah's expressions of worship were instituted immediately upon their deliverance from Egyptian slavery. In their worship, the people were vividly reminded of the God who loved them, who miraculously delivered them, and who promised to protect them. Their religious ceremonies and activities represented the very foundations and identity of the nation. But the worship that had once been a vibrant and meaningful focus upon God and His powerful love had degenerated into a ritualistic waste of time, for God would have nothing to do with it.

To compound the crisis, Isaiah informed the people that God not only rejected the religious rituals but that He actually despised these empty exercises. The Lord referred to their offerings as "meaningless" and "detestable" (v. 13). He called their religious assemblies "evil," declaring that He *hated* their gatherings and celebrations and that they were a burden to Him (vv. 13-14)! Finally, God announced that He hid His eyes from those who prayed and refused to listen to their prayers (v. 15).

Why would God be so enraged? What had the people done to provoke Him to such an impassioned response? Once again we are drawn to verse 17 and reminded of the nation's civil failure to maintain justice, relieve the oppressed, and defend the helpless. However, at this point we find that their neglect was not only civil failure but sin! Isaiah admonished them in verse 16 to *wash and make yourselves clean. Take your evil deeds out of my sight! Stop doing wrong.*

As we found in chapter 1, God gave the people of Judah a voice in determining their leaders, especially on a local level. According to God's earlier command, the people were responsible for appointing leaders who would be just, impartial, and free from greed (Deut. 16:18-20). However, their leaders had defied these civil standards, and in verse 16 Isaiah sets the burden of sin squarely upon the people. They had allowed unjust and sinful leaders into key positions, and while God indicted these leaders for their civil sin, He also accused the people for their neglect in the process. The people of Judah knew God's desire and design for government, and they could have influenced the leaders accordingly—but they did not. Thus, their neglect in overseeing the civil arena was sin.

We will take a closer look at verse 17 in chapter 3 and examine these three civil expectations more fully. In chapter 5 we will consider why God was so passionate about these civil sins. But for our purposes here we must understand that Isaiah clearly identified Judah's civil neglect as sin and that God passionately rejected their worship because of their civil sin.

As we've pointed out, Judah was guilty of additional sin that hindered their worship. Here, however, Isaiah directly connects God's rejection of their worship to the leaders' civil sin and to the people's sinful silence.

There is a tragic footnote to Isaiah's address to the people of Judah. God held back on His judgment for about 140 years before He allowed the Babylonian army to invade and utterly destroy Judah and her capital, Jerusalem. Many of the people were deported to Babylon where they lived in exile. Years later, God allowed some of the Jewish people to return to begin rebuilding the nation. When He did, He spoke through the prophet Zechariah, reminding them of His earlier expectations in civil matters.

Through Zechariah, he declared:

This is what the LORD Almighty says: "Administer true justice; show mercy and compassion to one another. Do not oppress the widow or the fatherless, the alien or the poor. In your hearts do not think evil of each other." But they refused to pay attention; stubbornly they turned their backs and stopped up their ears. They made their hearts as hard as flint and would not listen to the law or to the words that the LORD Almighty had sent by His Spirit through the earlier prophets. So the LORD Almighty was very angry. "When I called, they did not listen so when they called, I would not listen," says the LORD Almighty. "I scattered them with a whirlwind among all the nations where they were strangers" (Zech. 7:8-14).

Once again, we find a discourse that centers on Judah's civil failure. Because the people refused to hear and apply God's standards for government, God refused to hear their prayers. From God's viewpoint, Judah's civil failure (as shown by the leaders' activities and the people's negligence) was sin. As a result of their sin, God despised and rejected their worship.

A FAIR COMPARISON

It happened then, but could it be happening today in the United States? Could our ongoing failure to recognize and address the moral issues in the civil arena actually impact our worship?

In all fairness, we must recognize some of the major differences between Judah's worship then and ours today. First, Judah's worship was tied directly to her civil structure. As we've already indicated, Judah was a theocracy. God was her governmental head, and all leaders in the civil structure were expected to look to God and His Word for national direction. Within this theocracy, worship was essentially linked to the "state" and vice versa. If either the worship activity or the civil function failed to focus on God, both areas suffered. So when Judah's leaders rejected God's civil standards, they should not have been surprised when God rejected their worship.

Unlike Judah, the United States is not a theocracy and was never intended to be one. Our Founding Fathers didn't offer this model, and we have no indication from God that this was His desire. Therefore, there is no official, formal link between our nation's worship and our civil government.

A second difference regards the nature of Judah's worship. When God established the nation, He gave them a central location for worship and specific guidelines for sacrifices and various offerings. The people regularly brought animals to the temple to be sacrificed as payment for their sins. They also were expected to join in national festivals and celebrations that commemorated God's goodness to them.

Those of us who follow Christ understand and appreciate the Jewish heritage of worship, but we recognize that God has not established the same format of worship for us. We believe that Jesus was the promised Messiah who offered Himself as the ultimate and final sacrifice for sin. As a result, our celebrations focus upon His birth, death, and resurrection, and the forgiveness and new life He gives to those who repent and turn to Him. While we share a love for and a common heritage with our Jewish brothers and sisters, the form and focus of our worship is significantly different.

Therefore, in light of these differences some might say any comparison with Judah would be invalid. It may be true that Judah's civil sin (as reflected in the leaders' violations and the people's negligence) impacted their worship, but does it necessarily follow that our failure to address civil sins impacts our worship?

We asked a similar question in the last chapter, and here we have a similar response. Judah does not serve as a model for our government nor for our worship. Judah's experience does, however, offer an illustration of at least three spiritual principles that were at work then and have application for us today. Let's examine each of them and see how they impact the U.S.

Divine Expectations

The first principle at work in Judah's case is this: *God has basic requirements of all civil leaders; and when leaders fail to meet these standards, they sin and face God's judgment.* We briefly alluded to this in chapter 1, but the point applies even further in this discussion. God clearly demonstrates throughout Scripture that He is the ultimate source, and absolute authority over of *all* civil authority, and that He sets the standards for all civil authorities. Therefore, when any civil leader violates God's standards for government, that leader defies God and faces God's judgment.

It should be noted here that this accountability to God is not dependent upon the leader's religious beliefs. God holds the leader accountable for these standards whether or not that person believes in God. An elected official may try to dismiss this accountability by preaching the "separation of church and state," but it does not relieve him or her from Divine authority, expectations, and accountability.

Reality exists, whether or not a person chooses to believe reality. The reality is that God has clear, moral standards concerning government policy. He has made these standards available to all leaders through His Word. If a leader chooses to deny the reality of God's standards as offered in His Word, or if the leader knows these expectations and chooses to defy them, that leader sins and faces the prospect of God's judgment.

This principle was in effect in Isaiah's day; Judah's leaders defied God's civil priorities and were therefore guilty of sin. However,

39

elected and appointed civil leaders still fall under the same principle today. God still has basic civil standards, and when civil leaders deny or defy them, they sin.

"to him who knoweth to do good..."

The second principle pictured in the example of Judah is as follows: *When God's people know His basic moral standards for civil government, and when they have the legal opportunity to influence their civil leaders accordingly, and when they fail to do so (resulting in rampant civil sin), they themselves sin.* This principle was indeed at work in the theocratic structure of Judah, but it was not restricted to that civil structure. It also applies to any representative form of government, including the United States. We have open access to God's Word and can see His clear, specific, and undeniable expectations in the civil areas of justice, relief for the oppressed, and protection for the helpless (see chapter 3 for a detailed explanation of these three areas). God has not kept His desires and expectations secret. Also, each of us has open access to the legislative process and is able to influence government policy and decisions. So, when we know His desire but neglect the steps available to us to prevent massive civil immorality, we sin.

In coming chapters we'll look more closely at these standards, but for now we will illustrate the point with a hypothetical situation. Suppose a congressman sponsors a bill to legalize child prostitution. Based on the authority of Isaiah 1:17, we can be certain that God would abhor the resulting and inevitable massive victimization of helpless children. Yet, if we know His desire on the issue but don't take steps to contact our senators and representatives and insist that they block this bill, we would stand before God guilty of sin.

At least two passages from the New Testament support this point. The first is Jesus' call to His followers in Matthew 5:13-16 to be "salt" and "light" in the world. The passage calls the Lord's followers to have a positive, moral impact on our world, an impact that deters moral decay and addresses moral darkness. Jesus' intent was not merely for His followers to be salt and light through their words only, but also to address decay and darkness through their actions (v. 16).

One arena where U.S. citizens are able to apply salt and light is our civil structure. When we see government activity or policies that allow (or even advance) moral decay and darkness, we have a legitimate recourse available to restrict and eliminate that activity. Influencing government to uphold God's civil standards is merely applying salt and light to decay and darkness. When we fail to vote, or when we vote for a leader whose platform advances or allows moral decay and darkness, or when we fail to hold elected leaders accountable in these areas, we fail to function as salt and light. In other words, we disobey the Lord.

Another passage that reinforces the principle is James 4:17, which says: *Anyone, then, who knows the good he ought to do and doesn't do it, sins.* If we know that a governmental policy directly defies God's heart and His command, and if we are able to influence or prevent that policy through our vote and access to elected representatives, and when we fail to use the civil structure available to us to do so, we sin. Our duty—before God and our nation—requires that we find and vote for candidates who would oppose such a policy. It also requires us to energetically challenge our elected officials to oppose that policy. Taking these actions is merely the "good" we ought to do. When we fail to take these steps, we disobey the Lord.

Though we are not a theocracy as Judah was, the principle at work in Isaiah's day is still valid and applies to us today. When

God's people know His moral standards for governmental policies, and when we have the civil means available to prevent clear examples of civil immorality, and when we don't attempt to do so —we sin.

A Deaf Ear to Prayer

The third principle illustrated in Judah's example is this: *When people realize their sin and repeatedly refuse to turn from that sin, God rejects their worship.* Judah experienced this principle firsthand. Because of their ongoing civil sin, God rejected their worship. However, Isaiah's indictment is not the only passage that teaches the principle. Earlier, we referred to Psalm 66:17-18, where the Psalmist says: *I cried out to him with my mouth; His praise was on my tongue. If I had cherished sin in my heart, the Lord would not have listened.* These verses emphasize the same point—God does not receive the praise nor hear the prayers of those who knowingly and intentionally continue in sin.

A broader search of the Bible shows that the principle is not merely an Old Testament concept. Jesus alluded to the same principle in the Sermon on the Mount. Matthew 5:23-24 records His command to be reconciled with an angry brother before presenting an offering to the Lord. The circumstances are different, but the concept is the same: Our worship is unacceptable to the Lord when there is ongoing, undeniable sin in our lives.

Peter made the point to husbands, announcing that if they did not treat their wives properly, their prayers would be hindered (1 Pet. 3:7). The New Testament makes the same emphasis regarding an individual's fellowship with God (1 John 1:6-9; 3:21-22), as well as a church's combined relationship with God (Rev. 3:14-22). The Scripture is consistent throughout on the issue. When people continue to defy God and consistently reject His standards, their worship is virtually a waste of time, for God will not receive it.

As we combine these principles, we are confronted with this stark prospect: When our elected and appointed leaders continue to deny or defy God's moral civil standards, they sin and God rejects their worship. Furthermore, because ours is a representative form of government, if we, the people, know God's moral standards for government but continually allow our leaders to defy His standards, we sin and our worship is severely hindered.

The United States is not exempt from these truths. Our leaders are expected to keep God's standards, and we are expected to attempt to elect officials who will keep God's standards and attempt to replace officials who don't. We are also able (and therefore expected) to monitor and influence our elected officials according to these standards. When our elected officials propagate and implement policies that defy God's moral standards because we have failed in these two areas, we have sinned and face the prospect of worship that is null and void.

To answer the questions posed earlier: Yes, when we know God's heart on the moral issues in government, and when we consistently allow our leaders to spurn His civil standards (by our silence and absence in the civil arena), these failures *can* and *do* negatively impact our worship.

NATIONAL IMPLICATIONS

Considering the religious makeup of our nation, the potential ramifications are staggering!

Let's first examine some of the possible implications for our chosen leaders. How do these truths impact the prayer life and worship that takes place in civil settings? Consider all of the city and county commission meetings that open with prayer. What about the mayors, commissioners, governors, state senators and representatives, and national leaders all across our country who support and participate in the National Day of Prayer? Think about all of the House and Senate sessions that begin with prayer. What does this suggest about the various "prayer breakfasts" that take place among government officials?

We find our leaders in these settings routinely invoking God's blessing, guidance, and protection for our cities, counties, states, and nation. But, according to God's Word, if the people involved refuse to keep God's moral priorities for civil government, God will reject those prayers. Those requests for blessing, guidance, and protection will be ignored.

Suppose one of these leaders claims to be born again, yet he or she continues to endorse a policy that clearly opposes God's moral and civil standards. It makes no difference what the leader claims about his or her faith nor how often he or she attends church. As long as the leader continues down that path of open defiance, that person's worship and prayer are dramatically impacted.

Now, what if that person serves in a nationally strategic position and faces an international crisis that could threaten the security of the United States as well as the entire world? If that individual goes to God in prayer, pleading for wisdom, direction, and protection for the nation, there is no reason to expect God to answer that prayer. According to the passages and principles above, the person is basically on his or her own. The frightening reality is that the long-term safety and security of our nation is heavily impacted by this simple truth. When government leaders continue to deny or defy God's moral standards for civil government, they sin and God rejects their prayer and worship.

But what of our citizens? How do these principles impact the effectiveness of the religious activities across our nation?

According to statistics, over the last thirty years on average less than half of the eligible voters in this nation voted in general elections.[10] Even more alarming are statistics that indicate the percentages are about the same—and perhaps even less—for those who call themselves Christians.[11]

If this is the case, then the verdict for most worship in America is grim indeed. If the majority of Christians know God's heart on issues of civil immorality but continually refuse to address these civil sins through their vote and access to elected representatives, then it stands to reason that, according to the principles listed above, God would reject the majority of our worship in this nation!

This is an alarming prospect. What does this suggest about all of the religious activities mentioned earlier in this chapter? The majority of Americans pray, contribute to the church, and view themselves as having a relationship with God. But if those same folks understand God's heart on these matters, yet refuse to vote for candidates who will maintain God's civil standards, all of these activities may be wasted. And if these same people realize God's deep passion on these issues, but do not contact their elected representatives on the policies that defy God's priorities, God may reject their prayers, offerings, and attendance at church services. This may seem harsh, but what other viable conclusion can we draw?

Not only does this impact individuals, it also impacts the local church. If the majority of members in a local congregation understand God's concern but refuse to function as salt and light in the moral issues of the government, they should not be surprised if God rejects their worship services, prayer meetings, revival services, mission offerings, building-fund drives, Easter pageants,

Christmas pageants, evangelistic emphases, Sunday School emphases, and so on.

It should be no surprise when this church sees little or no change in the people's lifestyles, for God may not be hearing those prayers for spiritual renewal. The people should not expect to see growth in the congregation, for God may have already turned His back on the activities of that church. In fact, if we take the passage from Isaiah seriously, God actually despises these activities and is disgusted with these meaningless rituals when His people know His expectations but refuse to obey Him in the civil arena.

This would not be the first time God has shown His disgust for a church's inactivity. In Revelation 3:14-21 He warned the church in Laodicea that because they were "lukewarm" (complacent and indifferent to God's concerns), He was ready to spit them out of His mouth! A church whose members refuse to address God's moral priorities in civil government should be prepared for Him to respond in the same manner. When God has revealed His moral and civil priorities for government, and when people know these priorities but continually neglect them, their worship and prayer degenerate into empty, meaningless, and repulsive ritual before God.

The implications do not stop there. What of the pastors across this nation who hold the same perspective as Pastor Benson in the opening illustration? He had a strong policy of "not mixing politics and religion," feeling that the church was not the place to discuss government policies and political issues. He had members from both political parties in his congregation and did not want to divide the congregation or step on any toes. All the while, Gov. P.J. Bates and his administration were being swept away in a tide of greed and corruption, leaving the good people of the state floundering in the backwash.

When pastors know God's clear expectations in key issues of civil government, but they take a stance similar to Pastor Benson's, refusing to speak out against immoral governmental policies, they should not be surprised when they don't see God at work in the congregation. God never intended for us to withdraw from the civil arena, but instead to stand for His moral civil priorities. Sometimes standing for God's concerns will offend church members, but we are called to stand, nevertheless.

Finally, let's consider how these principles impact the religious denominations in our land. Christian denominations in the U.S. are spending hundreds of millions of dollars annually to advance the cause of Christ. What if God rejected most of these contributions and activities? It may seem extreme, but it certainly is plausible.

If the majority of churches and individuals who contribute to a denominational organization fail to obey the Lord's expectations in the civil arena, the consequences likely will be felt within the denominational organization. Furthermore, if the leaders appointed to serve the denomination fail to vote according to God's principles, or if they fail to hold their elected officials accountable, they also disobey the Lord and their denominational efforts are likely to be in vain. It makes no difference how many dollars are collected, how much material is mailed, how much training is provided, or how many emphases are made. If God's people knowingly and continually reject His priorities, the result of their religious activity is a monumental waste of time, energy, emotion, and money. Even worse, it is an offense to God.

One specific application in closing: Isaiah ended this section with a warning that spans the centuries and confronts us face to face. In verse 15 he indicated that God refused to hear His people's prayers because their hands were "full of blood."

The people and leaders of Judah were ignoring the destruction of innocent lives. We will deal with this more fully in the next chapter, but we must point out here that the most heinous example was the sacrifice of babies to the pagan deity Molech. Those who actually sacrificed their babies, as well as the pagan priests who helped them, had blood on their hands; the leaders who failed to enforce God's standards, thus allowing this carnage, had blood on their hands; and the people who failed to hold their leaders accountable to God's standards—those who remained silent in the face of such atrocities—had blood on their hands. Thus, God refused to hear their prayers.

When we consider the blight of abortion that plagues our nation, should we expect anything different today? Those who perform abortions have blood on their hands. The civil leaders who do not oppose the practice—our judges, as well as our legislators—have blood on their hands. And those of us who elect such leaders, or who fail to even vote, or who remain silent in the face of the ongoing slaughter, have blood on our hands. Therefore, how could we expect God to hear our prayers?

Of course, God always hears and responds positively to prayers of confession and repentance—but it seems our nation has forgotten how to pray this way.

CONCLUSION

The implications for our churches and our nation are alarming. When we choose to ignore violations of God's civil expectations, we sin. And when we insist on walking in sin, our worship is wasted.

We should not be surprised or dismayed at the spiritual poverty displayed throughout our nation and in our churches. Somewhere, somehow, we lost sight of God's priorities for our national leaders and for the citizens they represent. As we have become apathetic toward the moral issues inherent within government, as we have failed to hold our elected leaders accountable in these matters, as we have failed to vote, as we have gradually turned our backs on God's priorities in these areas, we should not be surprised if God has turned a deaf ear to our prayers.

It would not be fair to suggest that all churches across the land fall into this category. Many fine churches and pastors embrace God's civil priorities and promote an active, Christian citizenship.

Nor would it be fair to suggest that neglecting God's civil expectations is the only problem facing our churches today. In chapter 7 we will examine sins that often accompany the neglect of God's civil standards. Those sins plagued Judah, and they contribute to our dilemma today. But, while neglecting God's civil expectations may not be the only problem in U.S. churches today, the evidence is undeniable—this is a major stumbling block that must be removed if we hope to ever see revival in our land. Furthermore, based on the biblical record, if we don't deal with the issue, we need not look for God to receive our worship and prayers warmly, especially prayers for national deliverance and protection.

Hear once again God's Word through the prophet Zechariah: *"When I called, they would not listen; so when they called, I would not listen," says the LORD Almighty* (Zech. 7:13).

1. "Spiritual Progress Hard to Find in 2003," *The Barna Update*, December 22, 2003, www.barna.org/FlexPage.aspx?Page=BarnaUpdate&BarnaUpdateID=155.

2. "Religious Beliefs Remain Constant But Subgroups Are Quite Different." *The Barna Update*, March 19, 2004, http://www.barna.org/FlexPage.aspx?Page=BarnaUpdate&BarnaUpdateID=160.

3. Ibid.

4. "Church Attendance," *Barna By Topic*, www.barna.org/FlexPage.aspx?Page=Topic&TopicID=10.

5. "Stewardship," *Barna By Topic*, www.barna.org/FlexPage.aspx?Page=Topic&TopicID=36.

6. "Faith Commitment," *Barna By Topic*, www.barna.org/FlexPage.aspx?Page=Topic&TopicID=19.

7. William Bennett, "Executive Summary," *The Index of Leading Cultural Indicators 2001*, Empower.org, www.empower.org/execsumm.pdf.

8. "Teen Suicide," Focus Adolescent Services, www.focusas.com/Suicide.html.

9. "The State of our Unions 2003, The Social Health of Marriage in America," p. 23, produced by the National Marriage Project, at Rutgers the State University of New Jersey, http://marriage.rutgers.edu/Publications/SOOU/SOOU2003.pdf.

10. According to the Strategic Information and Planning Section of LifeWay Christian Resources.

11. William Bennett, The Index of Leading Cultural Indicators 2001, Empower.org, 171

12. According to the University of Akron's Bliss Institute of Applied Politics, per a conversation with director John Green.

Chapter 3

RAISING THE STANDARD

Billings cursed his putter as he flung it into the leather golf bag strapped to the rear of his cart. Earlier in the game he might have been more discreet, but disgust at his poor performance on the 14th hole replaced any concern for appearances. He knew the grain and every break on that green better than he knew his own office. There was no way he should have missed such an easy shot. To make matters worse, Beasley's birdie putt had just placed him two strokes ahead. John Billings was appalled by the thought of losing at anything, but the prospect of losing a round of golf to a defense attorney was more than he could stomach.

For most people, the pampered, pastoral setting of this course would offset feelings of tension or anger. At every hole, golfers are greeted by finely manicured fairways and greens. Each tee is surrounded by multicolored and meticulously groomed flowerbeds. The lush trees throughout the course are sanctuary to thousands of birds that regularly serenaded the golfers. The Meadowbrook Country Club is admired and recognized throughout the land as home to this premier course. Membership at the very expensive and exclusive club is one of the "trophies" awarded to those in high government positions.

Billings liked it here. He wasn't bothered by criticism leveled at the club for not welcoming "minority" members. Since his business dealings and policies had greatly benefited minorities (which had, ironically, advanced his own career and made membership at this club a reality) he felt no obligation to share the course with any of them.

Beasley had watched the failed putt from a safe distance and had already climbed into the cart by the time Billings speared the golf bag with his club. As Billings stormed up to the driver's side and dropped behind the wheel, Beasley politely pretended not to notice the tantrum and made a conciliatory remark about his own luck at the hole, which only fanned the flames of Billings's anger.

Michael Beasley's polished golf game was a reflection of his own legal career. There was no sacrifice too great to become the best. He invited challenge and flourished under pressure. He selected his opposition carefully, so victory was the norm and defeat the exception. He could calmly adapt himself to any and every circumstance and could apply either force or finesse as needed. After only brief observation, he could size up his challenger's strengths and weaknesses and use both to his own advantage. Partners admired his style, and opponents feared his next stroke.

When John Billings heard the first rumblings of an indictment, he anxiously asked around for the very best defense attorney. Beasley's name surfaced repeatedly. He was warned that Beasley was high caliber and, consequently, high priced, but Billings learned early in his construction business that "you get what you pay for."

As Billings started the cart toward the next hole, he shook off his rage and resumed their previous conversation, "Mike, let me make sure I understand you. Are you saying that my guilt or innocence may have nothing to do with the outcome of this case?"

"I wouldn't choose to phrase it that way," Beasley replied, "but based upon my preliminary review, our strategy will be to get the judge to drop the case. It appears that one of our state's "finest" may have overstepped the boundaries in his investigation. If we can verify that, the charges should be dropped entirely."

As they wheeled around the curve and under the huge oak, Billings felt the knot in his stomach ease slightly. He had been confident all along that he would be able to beat the charges. His past had taught him the art of fighting to win, and from the battlefields of big business he knew that there was *always* a way to prevail. He was mentally prepared to do whatever was necessary in order to conquer his newest enemy, so he was pleasantly surprised at the prospect of a quick victory.

"However," Beasley added, "this will require extensive research. If we're going to do this right, it *will* get expensive."

Billings thought for a moment. Off the top of his head, he counted eight businessmen who owed him favors. They had good reason for wanting Billings to continue as Secretary of Housing and would be generous in their financial support. Of course, he would have to establish the proper fund for their donations, but he could work out those details later.

"That won't be a problem," he answered. "You just go ahead and do whatever you need to do to get me past this. I've got projects waiting for me, and I can't be distracted by this (expletive deleted) anymore."

Armed with new resolve, Billings pulled up to the 15th tee, set the parking brake on the cart, and pulled out his *Big Bertha*. He set his ball and tee and took his stance, determined to intimidate Beasley with this drive and regain control of the game.

If this conversation were uncommon, our nation might have less cause for alarm. But, while the account is fictitious, similar discussions have been repeated countless times in countless settings. As we track court proceedings in the news media, we are dismayed at the obvious link between financial means and a quality legal defense. We deplore accounts of officials whose policies buy, and are bought by, "favors." The image is inescapable. It appears that our nation's legal and political direction is determined more by financial influence than by just laws and moral standards.

Yet, in addition to the growing link between finances and "justice," the opening illustration raises a second concern. In our story line, Billings is actually guilty of using his position to funnel government contracts to his business. He *should* suffer appropriate consequences for such an abuse of power, but the indications are that the charges will be dropped. And, even if they aren't dropped, few would expect him to pay significantly for his crime.

It seems that society no longer expects serious consequences for illegal behavior. The concept of "punishing" a criminal for his crime seems to have been replaced with excusing or explaining his behavior. Our collective focus seems to have shifted from the criminal "act" to the circumstances surrounding the action. The nation voices alarm at the increase in crimes, but what are we doing to deter criminal behavior?

A third concern that surfaces from this story is John Billings's flagrant racism. He viewed "minorities" as no more than a professional obligation at best and pawns for his own career advancement at worst. His primary focus as a public servant was not on protecting the helpless and caring for those in need, but on using the needy for his own purposes. However, Billings is not the first public servant to use the needs of others to advance a political career, is he?

The scenario is all too common, and the realities pictured are deplorable. But what response, if any, should Christians have to similar political and governmental conditions in the United States? We've seen in the first two chapters that God holds the people accountable for the civil sins of their appointed leaders and that Christians' failure to follow through with civil responsibilities can hinder worship. But the evidence of these two chapters alone may not be enough to convince us. The question still remains: What does God expect of us as eternal Kingdom citizens who live in a temporal, earthly kingdom? Is there more Biblical evidence that calls us to a clear stand for civil morality in the U.S. government? Or should we simply concede the fact that unsaved politicians will inevitably behave as unsaved politicians, and restrict our spiritual energies to the clearer priority of proclaiming the good news of the gospel?

Timely questions, indeed—which takes us back to God's Word as revealed through our good friend, Isaiah.

GOD'S WORD

So far we've seen Isaiah's shocking indictment of the leaders and people of Judah in 1:10, and his alarming announcement concerning their wasted worship in verses 11-16.

But now, as we consider the truth of verse 17, we find the source of God's scathing rebuke in previous verses. Here Isaiah declares: *Learn to do right! Seek justice, encourage the oppressed. Defend the cause of the fatherless, plead the case of the widow.*

In this brief but intense command Isaiah reveals the fuel of God's fiery denunciation. Here he summarizes both the expectation and the failure of God's people in three areas that were foundational for their relationship with Him and each other.

Because of the activities taking place in the government, as well as in the general population, a citizen of Judah could have grasped the urgency of these commands as well as the depths of their own failures. Yet if today's Christian citizen were to consider these few statements alone, that person would not appreciate the evidence presented in God's survey of Judah's civil failures. We cannot appreciate the level of God's expectation nor the gravity of Judah's failure unless we examine these verses against the larger backdrop of God's Word and the history surrounding Judah at the time.

Seek Justice

Following His rebuke in the previous verses, God admonished the people to "learn to do right!" Then He summarized His expectations with four positive commands. The first command was for the leaders and people of Judah to "seek justice." The concept behind the term "justice" included far more than what we can cover here. We will, however, consider some of the primary principles behind Isaiah's use of the term, as well as some key areas of application.

Right and Wrong

In Isaiah's writings the concept of justice was supported by at least three key principles. The first was that God expected justice to be firmly grounded upon moral standards of right and wrong that flowed out of His character. In Isaiah 5:20, He scolded Judah for replacing "good" with "evil," "light" with "darkness," and "sweetness" with "bitterness." The accusation applied to several sinful areas, but especially to civil immorality. Isaiah's prophetic contemporaries, Micah and Amos, addressed the same issues in both Judah and Israel (Mic. 3:2-11; Amos 5:7-15). Together they reveal a justice system that had redefined God's standards of right and wrong to suit their own desires. The concept of "right and wrong" in this system of justice included these three elements.

FAIRNESS

When God originally delivered His people from Egyptian slavery and led them to Mt. Sinai, He instituted clear civil laws to ensure fair business dealings. Moses wrote in Leviticus that they were not to defraud their neighbors or withhold wages from an employee (19:13). God was careful to protect His people from the dangers of unscrupulous businessmen. However, in Isaiah's time, the justice system saw nothing wrong with the practice of defrauding the poor and confiscating their land (Isa. 5:8,9; Mic. 2:1,2,9). What was previously "bitter" was now "sweet."

SEXUAL MORALITY

Following Israel's exodus from Egypt, God took steps to protect them from the self-destructive practices of the Canaanites, commanding them to reject their rampant and perverted sexual practices. Through Moses, God forbade His people from practicing any form of adultery, incest, homosexuality, or bestiality, all of which defied God's natural design (Lev. 18:1-23; 20:10-21).

Yet during the time of Isaiah, the people had achieved an "enlightened" perspective of human sexuality and were no longer enslaved by archaic and prudish constraints that frustrated and repressed their true, inner selves. Having liberated themselves from the shackles of religious intolerance, they were free to openly choose and express their sexuality (heterosexual, homosexual, or otherwise) with no fear of religious or civil interference. Thus, that which God had declared "darkness" had become "light."

PRECIOUS LIFE

As God prepared His people at Mt. Sinai, He repeatedly emphasized the value of human life and established laws forbidding murder (Ex. 20:13; 21:12-14,23,28-29). God's regard for life was clearly at work when He warned them of yet another Canaanite practice to be despised and avoided at any cost. In Leviticus 18:21, God commanded them: *Do not give any of your children to be sacrificed to Molech.* One of the groups inhabiting Canaan at the time was the Ammonites. Their favorite god was named Molech (the name meant "King"), and their worship included offering infants as burnt sacrifices to this pagan deity. The practice was detestable to God, and He warned His people to abhor and reject this abomination.

However, approximately six hundred years later, King Solomon reintroduced Molech to the people. For years he gradually had been turning from God's commands while turning to various pagan deities. God's Word tells us that Solomon set up a worship center for Molech on the east side of Jerusalem and began to worship and offer sacrifices to him, as well as to other pagan gods and goddesses (1 Kings 11:4-8). We're not certain if he sacrificed any children, but his actions at least set the stage for future atrocities.

About two hundred years later, during the ministry of Isaiah, King Ahaz ruled over Judah. God's Word reports that Ahaz was wicked and rejected God's commands outright. He set a hideous example for the people of Judah by offering his own child as a burnt sacrifice to Molech (2 Kings 16:3). The practice soon became accepted (2 Kings 17:17; Jeremiah 32:35), and future kings followed in the steps of Ahaz (2 Kings 21:6).

The actual procedure was gruesome and unimaginably cruel. Early accounts record that the living baby was removed from the parents' hands by Molech's priest and offered alive into the fiery arms of Molech, while deafening drumbeats shielded the parents from their child's screams.[1]

All the while, this grotesque abomination received legal and religious protection. That which had been "evil" had now become "good."

When God addressed His people through Isaiah, their moral foundations had eroded to the point that God's preordained standards of right and wrong no longer set the parameters for justice. They had been replaced with the corrupted desires of the day. For the people to "seek justice," they would have to return to the standards of good and evil that flowed from the loving heart of God, not from the degenerate mind of man.

Favor-Free Decisions

The second principle at work in Isaiah's emphasis on justice was in the realm of "gifts" and "favors" for civil leaders. The nature of justice (as God defined it) required judges and leaders to distance themselves from the lure of personal and financial gain that could influence their civil and legal decisions.

God was very specific and emphatic on this issue. When He gave His law through Moses, He was careful to forbid the influence of legal decisions through gifts (Ex. 23:8). And, as we emphasized in chapter 1, the Jewish people were commanded to choose leaders who would not receive or be influenced by bribes (Deut. 16:19). God knew that these favors would blind the leaders to truth and lead to unjust laws and rulings.

Unfortunately, in Isaiah's day the civil structure was driven by greed and acquisition. In Isaiah 1:23 the prophet uncovers political corruption in its rawest form. Those who were supposed to be guarding God's standards of justice were instead chasing after bribes and gifts. He went on to point out that these civil servants were acquitting "the guilty for a bribe" while denying "justice to the innocent" (5:23). There was a direct and deplorable correlation between financial means and legal decisions. This defied God's civil design in which laws and litigation were to be driven by that which was right, not that which was advantageous.

Isaiah challenged the outrageous actions of rich landowners who used their wealth to manipulate the system (Isa. 3:13-15; 5:8; Micah 2:2,9). He confronted the judicial travesty of allowing those who had shed innocent blood to be acquitted because of a fat bank account (Isa. 1:16; 5:7; 59:3-9; Mic. 7:2,3). He chastised leaders who focused on gain rather than impartial litigation (Isa. 1:23; 5:23; 33:15). And as he did, he reminded the people that to "seek justice" meant to divorce the legal process from financial influence.

Crime and Punishment

The third principle behind Isaiah's emphasis on justice concerned the issue of crime and punishment. The very nature of justice demanded appropriate punishment for those who violated God's standards. But in Isaiah's day, criminals didn't necessarily fear the prospect of civil discipline.

When we go back to Mt. Sinai and God's preparation of His people, we find that God was careful to include fitting punishment for violations. In some situations, violators were to provide restitution for the victims of their crimes (Ex. 22:1-14). However, some crimes warranted the death penalty (21:12-17; Lev. 20:1-16).

But the wealthy in Isaiah's time could defraud the poor without regard for the consequences (Isa. 5:8,9; Mic. 2:1,2,9). Those who were guilty of vicious and brutal crimes didn't necessarily face the proper penalties for their crimes (Isa. 59:1-9). The murder of innocent children in the name of a pagan deity was allowed, if not encouraged, with no fear of retribution. Justice requires a penalty for crimes, but in Judah there were no consistent penalties for crimes—thus there was no justice.

The broad concept of biblical justice involved far more than what we have covered here. For Isaiah, however, establishing true justice required the civil structure of Judah to maintain clear, God-ordained standards of right and wrong, to remove financial influence from the civil process, and to execute appropriate punishment for those guilty of breaking the law.

Three Primary Arenas

For us to further appreciate God's command through Isaiah, we must recognize the three civil areas where God expected justice to be "fleshed out."

First, God expected all of the civil leaders of Judah to maintain and protect justice. The word for "ruler" (NIV) in 1:10 and 23 was the same as the word for "judge," but the office and title weres not restricted to a judicial function. It was a broad term that applied to general leadership in the land, including military officers, governors, and kings.[2]

In God's civil design, He expected these civil leaders to set the example in the land by pursuing and protecting justice. For Judah to survive, her leaders would have to be personally committed to the concepts of keeping God's moral standards, separating financial influence from the civil process, and appropriate penalties for criminals (Deut. 1:9-18; 16:18-20; 17:14-20).

Yet, as we have seen, the leaders of Judah had forsaken God's expectations of justice. They were pictured as immoral, rebellious, thieving, greedy, evil, and corrupt conspirators (Isa. 1:10; 1:23; Mic. 3:1,2,9; 7:3). Rather than protecting justice, they were among the first to ravage the integrity of justice. When the people looked at their civil leaders, they didn't see sterling examples of justice, but the most sexually immoral, deceitful, and greedy individuals in the land. God's design for civil justice cannot survive in such a setting.

Second, God's expectations for civil justice went beyond the leaders. He also expected judges to dispense justice through their rulings in the cases that came before them. When victims brought their cases before the court, they should have found protection and relief. When a man was falsely accused, he should have received a fair hearing.

Instead, the courts of Judah had reversed God's design. The guilty were acquitted and the innocent convicted (Isa. 5:23; 29:21). The judges in these cases had long since forgotten God's moral standards, they had been totally corrupted by the lure of personal gain, and they had no concern whatsoever for seeing criminals punished for their crimes. Again, civil justice, as God defined it, cannot overcome such obstacles.

Finally, in addition to the leadership and courts of Judah, God expected justice to be displayed through those who actually wrote laws and ordinances.[3] Those who led and served as judges in Judah were in a position on occasion to establish or clarify certain laws. But when these individuals were not constrained by God's moral standards, and when they were influenced by the prospect of personal gain, the result was the establishment of legislation that was unjust and oppressive to certain people. This defied God's expectations for justice. Once again, this type of environment strangles God's design for civil justice.

When God established a civil design for His people, He was careful to protect the fledgling nation by weaving sound principles of justice into that design. God knew that if His people would follow these principles, they would be spared the societal suicide that accompanies a decline in moral standards, they would be delivered from the terminal corruption associated with "gifts," and they would be sheltered from the devastating societal chaos that follows unpunished crime. The leaders, judges, and lawmakers of the land should have been the first to have upheld these principles. Instead they compromised the executive, judicial, and legislative functions of their government when they replaced God's design with their own.[4]

Yet God in His love and mercy gave His people another chance to turn from their self-appointed path of destruction. Through the fiery voice of His committed spokesman, Isaiah, He challenged the people of Judah to turn from their rebellion and once again "seek justice."

Relieve the Oppressed

Isaiah continued with three additional commands that logically flow out of God's concern for justice. Whenever justice fails, there are victims, and the following commands focus on the needs of those victims.

The next command called the leaders and people to "encourage the oppressed" (or "relieve the oppressed," KJV).[5] When Isaiah relayed this mandate, he could have had at least two different groups of oppressed people in mind. The first group was the poor who had been abused by the rich. He rebuked the leaders of Judah for plundering and crushing the poor (3:14-15). As we have seen from 10:1, Isaiah also indicted the rich who had deprived the poor of their rights.

But we get a broader picture of the problem from Isaiah's contemporary, Micah, who addressed the same people and the same problems. In his writings, we find a charge against the rich who had seized the land and homes of Judah's poor (Mic. 2:2).

God's original design for His people provided that a family's property was to be their permanent possession, passed down from generation to generation. If, however, a landowner got into financial trouble, he could offer his land as payment for his debts. The new owner could then produce enough crops from the land to pay off the original debt. But eventually, after the debt was paid, the land had to be returned to the original owner so that his children would have a guaranteed inheritance and means of income.[6]

The rich in Isaiah's day, however, were far more concerned about the "bottom line" than about God's design. And they held the civil leaders and judges safely in their "deep pockets." When the poor attempted to take the rich landowners to court, the corrupt courts and civil leaders sided with the wealthy, and the poor had no legal recourse. Consequently, God in His concern and compassion for these victims stood as their Advocate and boldly demanded relief from their oppressors.

In addition to the needs of the poor, God also showed a special concern for those who were victims of violent crimes. He accused the worshipers of raising bloodstained hands in prayer and accused some of shedding innocent blood (Isa 1:15; 59:7; Mic. 7:2). These references seem to picture a general condition of widespread violence in the land. Victims suffered at the hands of the ruthless, but because money could buy acquittal, the victims had no legal recourse. However, God was deeply concerned for those who suffered unjustly, so He stood in their defense and cried for relief.

Beyond the picture of general violence was the specific travesty of child sacrifice to the pagan god Molech. As we've discussed, the atrocious act defiled the very heart of God's principles of justice. But in addition to God's call for specific civil standards, we also see a glimpse of God's deep compassion for those who suffered mercilessly at the hands of adults who chose to ignore God's timeless principles. These precious, innocent victims were allowed to be murdered; yet the adults would never have called it by that name. They chose to think of it in more noble and acceptable terms and justified it in their own minds by focusing on the perceived personal and national benefits that would result.[7] And the act was entirely legal!

Isaiah's writings do not indicate that all of the people were participating in the practice. It's likely that many if not most of the people disapproved of the pagan practice. However, they permitted the practice by not calling on their leaders to forbid these atrocities. God, on the other hand, would not sit idly by. Through Isaiah, He boldly and passionately demanded relief for these innocent victims of violence.

For the people of Judah to return to God and His protective design for them, they first had to renew their commitment to justice. And regaining a clear focus on justice required a concern for the victims of legal oppression. God's concern was not merely for a sound civil structure but also for the people who were supposed to be served by that structure. And so, as He called His people to "seek justice," He quickly followed with the command to "relieve the oppressed."

Defend the Helpless

The final two commands of verse 17 further illustrate God's loving focus on those who were supposed to be served by justice. Through Isaiah God directs the people of Judah to "defend the cause of the fatherless, plead the case of the widow."

God's focus on these two groups (orphans and widows) demonstrates both His concern for them and their particular plight during the time of Isaiah. When God established His principles of justice, they included the concept of individual "rights." Each individual in Judah was due fair treatment and protection through the civil structure.[8] If a citizen of Judah had been treated unfairly or had suffered at the hands of the ruthless, he could appeal to the civil authorities for relief and protection.

Sadly, that process often broke down in the cases of orphans and widows. For generations, neighboring cultures had restricted the focus of their respect to the men of the land. In these male-dominated societies women and children were dependent upon the men for both food and protection. Apart from the security of a husband and father, widows and orphans were defenseless against the ravages of brutal human predators. In essence, they had no legal voice and were denied individual human rights.[9]

But God knew of this potential neglect and abuse. As He prepared His people for life in Canaan, He was careful to specifically and intentionally address the needs of all women and children, but especially orphans and widows. He commanded the nation to provide for their needs and protect them from injustices (Ex. 22:22-24; Deut. 14:29; 24:17-21). By addressing these potential victims, He acknowledged their God-given rights that were to be protected by the civil structure. God's loving design transcended the male-dominated cultures of the day and granted widows and orphans a legal voice when faced with injustices.

Tragically, when Judah rejected God's design and embraced neighboring practices, God's concern for orphans and widows was ignored. What God warned against had become reality in Judah, and this unprotected group no longer had a legal voice. Their right to justice was no longer protected, and they were helpless under the attack of the ruthless (Isa. 1:23; 10:1,2). Greedy and unscrupulous businessmen could use and abuse them at will with no fear of legal action. They were no longer precious and protected individuals as God viewed them, but expendable pawns in a financial contest to be shuffled and spent as the "bottom line" dictated.

Once again God comes to the aid of the victim, demanding legal protection for these orphans and widows. He called for the leaders and courts of the land to stand in defense of the helpless. And as they did, they would once more reflect the true nature of justice as God intended it to be.

Verse 17 of Isaiah's first chapter is relatively small in size. Yet these few words provide a glimpse into the heart and passion of a loving God who will not ignore injustice. Through Isaiah, He called His people to return to the principles and application of true justice.

Showing more than a concern for principles and application, this verse also demonstrates God's passion for those overlooked in a corrupt civil system. He called on the leaders of Judah to relieve those who had been oppressed and to defend those who were legally helpless.

So we see a portion of the big picture at work in the passage. With this background before us it is easier to understand the shared guilt emphasized in verse 10. The people knew God's expectations and could have taken their leaders to task over these injustices. But they didn't, so they were jointly accountable. We can also appreciate why God would reject their worship in verses 11-16. They knew God's design and desire, but they would not keep either; therefore, their insincere worship was a waste of time and an offense to God. Yet in this verse God offered them another chance and called both the people and the civil leaders to return to His standards and applications of justice.

Still, we've not dealt with the matter of God's desire for Christian Americans and their proper response to present-day civil immoralities. It may be obvious that God was offended by the actions and activities of His people in Judah, but that was more than 2700 years ago. The events we've discussed may indeed be historically accurate and reflect God's passion regarding a specific situation at a specific point in time. But we are not in an identical situation, nor are we at that point in history. So why would we even consider God's relationship with Judah's government in the same context as the civil leadership and activities of the United States?

To answer that question, in chapter 4 we will examine our current civil condition and compare it to that of Judah. Then, in chapter 5, we'll consider it against an even broader backdrop. At that point we will see God's desire for us as Christian citizens in a non-Christian civil setting.

1. Robert Culver. "Molech," *Theological Wordbook of the Old Testament*, R. Laird Harris, editor, vol. 1, (Chicago: Moody Press, 1980), 509-510.

2. Willliam Gesenius. *A Hebrew and English Lexicon of the Old Testament*, edited by Francis Brown, S.R. Driver, and Charles Briggs, (Oxford: Clarendon Press), 1047-1048. Volkmar Herntrich: "shapat," *Theological Dictionary of the New Testament*, Gerhard Kittel, editor, vol. 3, (Grand Rapids: Wm. B. Eerdmans Publishing Company, 1977), 923-924;.Culver. *Theological Wordbook of the Old Testament*, vol. 2, 947-949.

3. Is. 10:1; also Jack P. Lewis, "haqaq," *Theological Wordbook of the Old Testament*, Vol. I, 316,317; "haqaq," *A Hebrew and English Lexicon of the Old Testament*, 349.

4. This is not to suggest that their govt. was divided into these three distinct and separate branches. It wasn't. Instead, each of these functions was combined into the various leaders/judges. Consider Culver's comments in *Theological Wordbook of the Old Testament*, 947-949 where he demonstrates that the concept of "judging" included the judicial function as well as the executive and legislative functions.

5. Actually, there is some debate among scholars over the correct translation of this phrase. Some feel that it should instead be translated "rebuke the oppressor" (as in the NASB and in the footnote of the NIV). There is good support for either translation, and in fact, both ideas may be satisfied in this command. To encourage (or "relieve" as it is translated in the *King James Version*) the oppressed requires a proper legal response to the oppressor. And, to rebuke the oppressor is to relieve the oppressed. However, because we have already dealt with the issue of punishing criminals, the focus of this discussion is on the needs of the oppressed individuals in Judah.

6. The observance of "jubilee" was to guarantee this return to the original owners. c.f. Lev.25:10-13; also, Num 27:1-11.

7. They thought of it in religious terms, thinking that such a sacrifice would please their spiritual "king" and bring his blessings. See Culver, Ibid.

8. See Is.10:2, 40:27(NASB) and 49:4(NASB). Also consider "mishpat," *A Hebrew and English Lexicon of the Old Testament*, 1049, #5; "mishpat," *Theological Wordbook of the Old Testament*, vol. 2, 949, #13.

9. John Pridmore, "Orphan," *Dictionary of New Testament Theology*, Colin Brown general editor, vol 2 (Grand Rapids: Zondervan Publishing House, 182), 737; Robert L. Hubbard, Jr., *The Book of Ruth*, (Grand Rapids: William B. Eerdmans Publsihing Company, 1988), 96-97.

Chapter 4

RAZING THE STANDARD

Nancy Jenkins slammed her legal pad down beside the computer on her desk. In her twenty-two years as a newspaper reporter, she couldn't remember being this frustrated. Bobby Landers, her partner, had just broken the news that John Billings had retained Michael Beasley as his defense attorney. She paced back and forth inside her ten-by-ten office cubicle, trying to think of a way around this devastating development, but she knew it was virtually hopeless. Beasley was the best, and everyone knew it. No matter what happened or how long it took, one way or another she knew that Billings would walk. If (more likely *when*) that happened, the fruit of the yearlong effort she had devoted to investigating and reporting this story would be reduced to fodder for the paper shredder. The frustration started to overwhelm her.

When Nancy began her career as a naive, fledgling reporter, she was committed to presenting the facts in unadulterated form. Her mentors had successfully convinced her of the need for journalistic ethics and integrity, and she had carried those convictions with her into every assignment. Jenkins had repeatedly faced and conquered the temptations of "editorializing" and "slanting stories." And as she experienced victories in each of these battles, she developed a deepening hunger for the truth.

The hunger grew into a crusade that led her into investigative reporting. She avoided stories that fed the public's appetite for scandal, but focused instead on incidents in which people clearly had been victimized. She was a sucker for the underdog, and her heart ached for those who had been abused by the powerful, the ruthless, and the greedy of society. Over the years she had earned a reputation for accuracy, integrity, and tenacity, and little pleased her more than to see the guilty brought to justice.

Which is why she had been interested in the early rumors about John Billings, the Secretary of Housing. About eighteen months after Governor Bates took office and appointed Billings to the position, Nancy got an anonymous phone call from a man who identified himself as a contractor in the southern part of the state. He said that Billings's old construction company had landed a lucrative state contract. She didn't think much of it at the time, but six months later she got a similar call from a different source.

That's when she began to dig. After some checking, she discovered that right after Billings had taken office, he initiated the formation of a minority controlled "shell" company. She then found that "coincidentally," the Department of Housing had awarded the contract for a low-income housing project to this new company, which in turn had subcontracted most of the work to his old company.

Billings, of course, had resigned from his position as CEO of the company, but when Nancy did some searching, she found that he was still a major stockholder. At that point she turned the information over to the authorities, confident that justice would be served. What she didn't expect was for Beasley to be thrown into the equation.

Nancy Jenkins's hopes for justice in this case had crashed and burned on the briefcase of a high-priced defense attorney. As she dropped into her chair and stared into the computer's blank screen, she wondered if it was too late to do anything.

Maybe I should forget about all of this and just cover stories from now on, she thought. *What's the use? Why should I beat my head against the wall? Maybe I'll go to work for a supermarket tabloid. People seem to care about those stories.*

She stood, grabbed her purse, and left her office. "Justice isn't blind," she muttered. "It's dead!"

Is Nancy Jenkins right? Has the justice system in this country deteriorated to the point that money determines innocence or guilt? It's a sobering prospect, but could it be that our nation has fallen to the same depths as Judah during Isaiah's day? In chapter 3 we saw that Judah had defied God's civil priorities of justice, relief for the oppressed, and protection for the helpless. Is it possible that our nation has also failed God's test in these areas?

Though separated by thousands of years and thousands of miles, there are some striking similarities between ancient Judah and contemporary America. As a nation, Judah faced an array of moral and social issues that tested its citizenry's commitment to the authority of God. Judah failed the test and thus incurred God's judgment.

Present-day America is confronted with many of the same issues and beset with many of the same problems that had been faced by the nation of Judah. America's response is not yet complete—but there are troubling signs that we too are racing down the same perilous path Judah had trod. Let's examine a few of our own civil standards to see how closely we compare.

SANCTITY OF LIFE

As we pointed out, part of God's standard for justice was His focus on the value of human life. Judah's citizens had displayed an utter disregard for the sanctity of innocent human life by sacrificing their children to a false god, Molech. The people were aided and abetted in this detestable practice by their kings, their priests, and others in authority. However, not unlike ancient Judah, present-day America also is sacrificing the lives of its future generations with the affirmation and approval of its civil authorities.

Abortion

In 1973, the U.S. Supreme Court decided the landmark case of *Roe v. Wade*. That case, along with the case of *Doe v. Bolton*, paved the way for abortion on demand in this country. Prior to those decisions, abortion was illegal, or at least restricted in some form, in every state in the union. The laws in all fifty states were effectively overturned, however, by the *Roe* and *Doe* decisions almost as soon as the decisions were rendered.

In arriving at its decision in *Roe*, the court ruled that the unborn child was not a *person* within the language and meaning of the Constitution. As a consequence, unborn children were stripped of all legal protection that *persons* enjoy under the Constitution. Reduced to *non-person* status, the court ruled that a mother's right to privacy outweighed her unborn baby's right to life, and only under the most limited of circumstances could the state interfere with a woman's "right" to choose an abortion. Subsequent cases have made it virtually impossible for the states to restrict abortion in any form, and today abortion is permissible for virtually any reason through the ninth month of pregnancy.

In the aftermath of *Roe v. Wade*, the lives of more than forty-two million unborn American children have been sacrificed on an altar of convenience to a false god named "Choice." These children perish at the rate of almost 4,000 per day. One out of almost every three children conceived in America dies at the hands of an abortionist.[1]

The brutality of the abortion procedures is mind boggling. Children in the womb are literally torn limb from limb by powerful suction machines. They are scalded or poisoned *in utero* by powerful and destructive chemical agents. And in the particularly gruesome "procedure" dubbed the "partial-birth abortion," the delivery of a nearly full-term child is interrupted temporarily so that her skull can be punctured and her brain sucked out. The skull is then crushed, and the delivery of the dead baby is thereafter accomplished. At the time of this publication, this procedure has been banned by legislation, but that legislation has not been enforced pending challenges in several states.

Not surprisingly, for many women who undergo abortion a lifetime of physical and emotional complications often follows.

Notwithstanding all of this, abortion on demand has persisted in America for over thirty years—thanks in no small part to the complacency and apathy of those who call themselves the people of God. While it is true that numbers of Christians, conscience stricken by the carnage, speak out against abortion, still more remain silent in the face of the cruelty and injustice that is meted out on unborn children. Many churchgoers have themselves procured or undergone abortions. Many pastors deny the Word of God on this subject and take a pro-abortion stance. Other pastors, fearful of offending the women in their pews or members who support pro-choice political candidates, are often mute when it comes to dealing with this polarizing issue. Taking their cues from their leaders in the pulpit, the laity often avoids the issue as well. As a result, the church has failed to forge the moral consensus that is necessary to eliminate the scourge of abortion from our land. The silence of Christians on this issue can only be deemed acquiescence to an abhorrent practice that callouses our nation's conscience and costs millions of our children their lives.

Biotechnology

Abortion is not the only practice sanctioned by the American government and its people that shows a lack of regard for the sanctity of the lives of creatures made in the image of God. Human cloning and embryonic stem cell "research" likewise devalue the *imago dei*. Both practices involve the deliberate creation and subsequent destruction of innocent human lives—usually justified by the pursuit of some "greater good" such as the quest for a medical "cure." What is rarely acknowledged, however, is that both practices require that a human being, admittedly quite small, must be killed in order to obtain the cure.

The small size of the embryo and the early stage of development are often cited by advocates of cloning and embryonic stem cell research as justifications for the practices. But size does not equate with significance, and age and maturity do not determine the worth of human beings. One cannot plausibly maintain that fat people are of more value than thin people or that the old are worth more than the young.

Our value as human beings stems from the fact that we are creatures made in God's image (Gen 1:27), and that His own Son shed His precious blood for us (1 John 2:2). Nevertheless, human cloning and human embryonic stem cell research are legal in the United States. In some instances, the research is even funded with taxpayer dollars. Here again, the church in America has largely been silent in the face of injustice, allowing these practices to not only continue but to proliferate.

Euthanasia and Elder Abuse

Euthanasia is another practice that has gained increased acceptance in America's justice system. "Mercy killing" has become so commonplace in America that Jack Kevorkian's suicide machine no longer makes the news. The state of Oregon has adopted legislation permitting assisted suicide and death advocates around the country clamor for the right to kill those whose quality of life fails to measure up to purely subjective standards. As this book goes to press one of its authors, Ken Connor, is defending "Terri's Law," pursuant to which Florida Governor Jeb Bush seeks to preserve the life of Terri Schiavo, notwithstanding a court order authorizing this handicapped woman's death by starvation and dehydration. Based on court rulings thus far, the prognosis for a successful defense of the statute is grim.

The same ethos that gives rise to the practice of euthanasia also contributes to the neglect of the weak and frail. Over a million people live in nursing homes in America, and many are the victims of abuse and neglect.[2] Large numbers suffer from preventable malnutrition, dehydration, and pressure sores. Many others are left to languish in their own waste, waiting helplessly for hours on end before someone comes to clean and change them. Aside from the unborn, no group suffers as much from the devaluation of human life in our society as the elderly.

The incidence of abuse and neglect in nursing homes is on the rise,[3] but rather than protecting our frail elderly and punishing those who cause them harm, many in government seek to immunize the wrongdoers from complete accountability for their conduct. Well-heeled lobbyists representing powerful nursing home interests regularly trump the rights of the frail elderly in the state capitals of America. All too often the needy and the vulnerable fare poorly in a system that is supposed to bring them justice. Like Judah, it appears that America's citizens and our government have lost sight of the high value God places on human life.

SANCTITY OF MARRIAGE

In ancient Judah the norms established by God for sexual behavior were commonly ignored and routinely violated. The same is indisputably true in America today, where the notion of containing sexual relations within the protective bounds of a monogamous heterosexual marriage is increasingly viewed as "prudish" and "antiquated" by our sexually liberated society. And, as with Judah, our civil leaders have provided protection for, and in some cases even endorsed this violation of God's civil standards.

Pornography

In modern America, sex sells! Our playboy generation uses sex to sell everything from toothpaste to toilet paper. Consumers are bombarded daily with images of sultry women and "buffed up" men hawking products guaranteed to increase one's sex appeal. But sex is not merely used indirectly to promote the sale of consumer goods; selling sex has become an end in itself.

Pornography generates $10 billion dollars each year in sales, more than the combined yearly revenues of all professional football, baseball, and basketball franchises, and greater than the annual take at all the nation's movie box offices.[4] Porn profits often fund organized crime enterprises.[5] Theaters that show X-rated films abound, and the number of adult bookstores have proliferated to the extent that they outnumber McDonald's restaurants in the United States.[6]

Pornographic "combat zones" exist in every large city in America. In these porn districts, virtually every product or service related to sex—nude dancing, prostitution, sexual paraphernalia, peep shows, and adult book and video stores—is available for willing consumers. The range of sexual goods and services is limited only by the imaginations of willing buyers and sellers. Consumers don't even need to leave their homes to obtain these products and services. "Sex talk" is readily available over the phone and is advertised on television. And for Internet surfers, any type of pornography is only a mouse click away.

Once again the courts of our land have helped facilitate the spread of these kinds of goods and services, often holding that they represent protected forms of speech or expression under the U. S. Constitution. Even attempts to shield children from exposure to obscene images over the Internet have been rebuffed by judges on First Amendment grounds. Sadly, the church also has become complicit in aiding and abetting the "sexual revolution." In city after city, clerics have been implicated in charges of pedophilia. The pervasive nature of the conduct and the extent to which church leaders have attempted to cover up the wrongdoing have rocked the foundations of at least one major denomination to the core.

Homosexuality

In the sexually charged atmosphere that often characterizes American life, homosexual behaviors have become increasingly open and accepted within the culture. In 2003, the U. S. Supreme Court, in *Lawrence v. Texas*, struck down a Texas statute that criminalized homosexual sodomy. The Massachusetts Supreme Court quickly followed with a decision that mandated same-sex "marriage" in that state. In cities around the country, mayors have authorized the performance of gay marriage ceremonies. Here again, the churches are complicit in these behaviors. Some denominations are ordaining openly homosexual clergy, while others solemnize homosexual relationships by extending to them the sacrament of marriage.

Homosexual activism has borne much fruit in the governmental arena. In a number of communities, governmental entities have voted to confer special rights on homosexuals. Disguised as "anti-discrimination" laws designed only to prevent unjust treatment of homosexuals in housing or hiring, the effect is often to accord preferential treatment to those who engage in homosexual behavior. Under such ordinances, a landlord can be forced to rent his garage apartment to a homosexual couple whose lifestyle he does not approve of and that he opposes on religious grounds. "Hate crimes" impose enhanced penalties for crimes directed at homosexuals, and laws that restrict adoption by homosexuals are increasingly being jettisoned.

Meanwhile, the sex education in our public schools conditions impressionable children to accept homosexual behavior as an acceptable "alternative lifestyle." Additionally, the "safe sex" emphasis that dominates much of today's sex education curriculum in public schools usually places homosexual sex on a par with heterosexual sex. The morality, or lack thereof, of pre- or extra-marital sex is rarely addressed, and the not-so-implicit message of the curriculum is that as long as one engages in "protected" sex, any kind of sex (heterosexual or homosexual) between consenting partners is OK.

One result of the changing sexual mores that are being fostered by the government is that sexual misconduct, once considered a liability for those seeking public office, no longer appears to be an impediment to government service. Barney Frank, a homosexual member of Congress who admitted to running a homosexual brothel out of his apartment, has regularly been reelected as a representative of the people of the state of Massachusetts. Former House Speaker Wilbur Mills was well known for his public escapades with a stripper. And Bill Clinton, whose sexual escapades were the topic of many nightly newscasts, is regarded as a political icon by many.

Judah ignored God's civil guidelines for sexual behavior. Tragically, it appears that our civil structure is following Judah's fatal example.

JUSTICE FOR SALE

Throughout the history of Israel, God warned His people of the corrupting influence of money on the administration of justice. Nevertheless, God indicted the nation of Judah for perverting justice through bribery. Matters were being decided by those in authority on the basis of money rather than the merits (Isa. 5:20,23).

Judicial Corruption

The effect of money on the administration of justice is no less pervasive and no less insidious in our day than it was in Judah's. Bribery cases have been prosecuted successfully to conviction throughout virtually every state in the United States. No branch of government at the local, state, or federal level has been spared the corrupting influence of graft within the system. The problem is so pervasive that the Justice Department (as well as many of its counterparts in the states) has a special section devoted exclusively to the prosecution of bribery and public corruption cases.

Within the judicial system there is a widespread perception that a double standard of justice exists—one for the poor and one for the rich. This perception is borne out by statistics that show that blacks and other minorities (who generally do not fare as well as whites on the economic scale) suffer stiffer sentences than whites for the very same crimes.[7]

Cases such as O.J. Simpson's have convinced many that money, rather than race, ultimately determines the outcome of a judicial proceeding. Wealthy defendants often spend vast sums in securing their acquittal. One is left to seriously question whether an accused charged with similar crimes, who lacked similar financial resources, would have obtained the same results.

Campaign Corruption

While the corrupting effects of illegal bribes are obvious, there are more subtle means by which America's system of justice is corrupted through the lawful payment of cash or other items of value. Political campaigns in America today are extraordinarily expensive. The cost of television and radio advertising has driven up costs so dramatically that one presidential candidate stated that "ready money" was the best friend a political candidate could have.[8]

In an effort to ingratiate themselves to political candidates, lobbyists and special interest groups often take the lead in raising money for candidates. Incumbent office holders (who are in the best position to accord favorable treatment to their donors) are the most common beneficiaries of these fund-raising efforts.

Even though there are usually limits on the amount of money an individual can contribute, political fund-raisers often avoid these limitations by a practice known as "bundling." Frequently, contributions will be made in the names of minor children, spouses, or others who may not be the actual source of the contributions.

Legislative Corruption

In addition to campaign contributions, professional lobbyists and special interests often wine and dine politicians and provide them with "perks" such as trips to expensive resorts, front row seats at premium sporting events, or hefty "speakers' fees" for addressing their interest groups. Of course, the lobbyists and politicians alike deny that such gifts or goods and services are calculated to influence the decisions of the office holder—which leaves one to wonder why such gifts usually stop only when the politician leaves office.

While denying that gifts influence decisions, lobbyists and politicians alike readily acknowledge that they do provide access for the lobbyists to the politicians. The clear implication is that those who do not provide such largess do not have access to their elected officials, a fact that the poor, and many who don't contribute monies to political campaigns, will affirm. The sad reality in America today is that far too often when it comes to obtaining justice in any arena of government, you only get what you pay for. A bribe by any other name is still a bribe, and its corrupting effect is no less pernicious in America in the twenty-first century than it was in ancient Judah.

RELIEVING THE OPPRESSED

Examples of how ordinary citizens are exploited by America's civil justice system abound. Because of the influence that powerful lobby groups exercise in the legislative arena, big business and other special interest groups are often able to limit the damages they have to pay when their negligence or wrongdoing causes harm to someone else. Favorable treatment obtained in the legislative arena often translates into favorable treatment in the judicial arena. Caps on damages, immunity from liability, shortened statutes of limitations for wrongdoing—all are examples of the preferred treatment that wealthy and powerful groups can acquire in America's justice system. Typically such preferred treatment translates into reduced protection in the judicial arena for those who are less wealthy and less powerful. Ordinary citizens frequently learn, only after they have suffered harm, that they have limited recourse (or perhaps none at all) against parties who have negligently or intentionally injured them. The prophet Isaiah warned against perverting the justice system by destroying the rights of individuals:

Woe to those who enact evil statutes, And to those who constantly record unjust decisions, So as to deprive the needy of justice, And rob the poor of My people of their rights, In order that widows may be their spoil, And that they may plunder the orphans (Isa. 10:1,2, NASB).

Nowhere does this appear more evident than in criminal sentencing. In today's environment, criminals often serve a mere fraction of the sentence imposed on them. Elaborately constructed programs of "gain time" often reduce the actual time served by a convicted felon to about half of the sentence imposed.[9] The U.S. Department of Justice reported that even though the median prison sentence for murder in 2000 was approximately twenty years, the average time estimated to be served by the convicted murderer would be only slightly more than thirteen years.[10]

One of the best examples of how the American government has victimized its citizens can be found in the welfare system. The Scriptures clearly impose an obligation on the part of those who have an abundance to provide for those who, through no fault of their own, are living in economic need. Thus the intent behind America's welfare system—to alleviate the needs of the nation's poor—is both scriptural and admirable. God may indeed expect our civil government to care for those who cannot properly provide for themselves.

Unfortunately, however, as crafted, America's welfare system often has fostered growing dependence on government by those who are economically disadvantaged. By taking away incentives to work and by immunizing people from the consequences of their own indolence or lack of responsibility, in many cases the welfare system has actually increased the number of people who are dependent on government for their survival. In addition, by providing insidious economic incentives to have children out of wedlock, the welfare system has been one of the biggest contributors to the breakdown of the two-parent family in America.

This is true even though single parenthood is one of the risk factors most often associated with juvenile delinquency, educational failure among children, teenage suicide, teenage pregnancies and teenage abortion. Additionally, the welfare system often victimizes the young by teaching them a flawed worldview. Children in the system sometimes grow up believing that one doesn't necessarily have to work to eat. Thus in its well-intended but sometimes misguided attempt to relieve America's poor of the often harsh results of economic need, the government has created a host of other problems that are far worse than those associated with poverty.

Those abuses that were present in Judah's justice system can be found in ours today. Sadly, our own government all too often mirrors Judah's disastrous example. If we are to achieve God's moral standards for civil government in American society, we must reach out and provide protection and relief for vulnerable groups who so desperately need our help, while encouraging those who are able to work to seek employment.

SOCIETY'S MORAL DECLINE

While moral decay often manifests itself in America's government, such decay is certainly not limited only to the government. Evidence that a general moral decline pervades the culture abounds. On May 25, 1987 *TIME* magazine asked this question in bold letters on its cover, "Whatever Happened to ETHICS?" It followed with this observation: "Assaulted by sleaze, scandals and hypocrisy, America searches for its moral bearings." The graphic on the cover showed a moral compass with a needle that pointed to neither right nor wrong. Few would disagree with the observation that cultural conditions have deteriorated in the meantime.

The sad reality is that in America today many have lost their way. Many have cut themselves loose from the moral moorings found in the Bible and the Jewish and Christian faiths. For such people, right and wrong no longer exist. It all depends. Relativism reigns. These people recognize no ultimate authority and affirm no ultimate truth. Along with Pontius Pilate, they cynically ask, "What is truth?"

Today's skeptics maintain that matters falling outside the realm of empirical verification—matters of morality and ethics—are at best matters of "opinion," with any one view being deemed as good (or bad) as another. Yet as former jurist and author Robert Bork observed, in a relativistic world, "One man's larceny is another's just distribution of goods."[11]

The attitudes expressed by America's secularists are summed up in the culture's clichés: "That may be right for you, but it's wrong for me"; "It doesn't matter what you believe as long as you sincerely believe it"; and "That may be your reality, but it is not mine." But the fruit of such reality has been an increase in divorce rates, sexually transmitted diseases, abortion, child and elder abuse, and crime.

In America, as was the case with Judah, there is no doubt that truth is in retreat and justice is in short supply. The evidence is compelling and suggests that, like Judah, our leaders and our nation have rejected God's expectations of justice, relief for the oppressed, and protection for the helpless. Our social foundations are crumbling beneath us. The question we must ask is, "Are we beyond repair?"

1. National Right to Life, "Trends and Statistics," www.nrlc.org/abortion/facts/abortionstats.html.

2. U.S. Census Bureau, "The 65 Years and Over Population: 2000, Census 2000 Brief," Table 8, www.census.gov/prod/2001pubs/c2kbr01-10.pdf.

3. Mark Thompson, "Shining A Light On Abuse," *Time*, Aug. 3, 1998.

4. Janet LaRue, "Porn Nation," *World and I*, Aug., 2001.

5. "Christian Involvement in Porn Benefits Organized Crime, A First-Person Perspective," By James L. Lambert, AFA Online, January 23, 2004, http://headlines.agapepress.org/archive/1/afa/232004c.asp.

6. As reported by Probe Ministries in the "The Pornography Plague," by Kerby Anderson, citing "Effect of Pornography on Women and Children," U.S. Senate Judiciary Committee, Subcommittee on Juvenile Justice, 98th Congress, 2nd Session, 1984, 227, www.leaderu.com/orgs/probe/docs/pornplag.html.

7. "State Court Sentencing of Convicted Felons, 2000," U.S. Department of Justice Office of Justice Programs, Bureau of Justice Statistics Special Report, www.ojp.usdoj.gov/bjs/pub/pdf/sc0002st.pdf, table 2.5.

8. Sen. Phil Gramm, as reported by Bruce Morton, "The big bucks are on Bush; now let's ask the people," *CNN.Com 1999 Year in Review*, www.cnn.com/SPECIALS/1999/yearinreview/field.reports/politics/.

9. "Criminal Sentencing Statistics," U.S. Department of Justice Office of Justice Programs, Bureau of Justice Statistics, http://www.ojp.usdoj.gov/bjs/sent.htm.

10. "State Court Sentencing of Convicted Felons, 2000," table 1.3, 1.5, www.ojp.usdoj.gov/bjs/pub/pdf/sc0001st.pdf.

11. "INSIGHT," *The Federalist: The Conservative e-Journal of Record*, 16 April 2003, http://www.federalist.com/pub/03-16_Chronicle.htm.

Chapter 5

RESTORING THE STANDARD

Barbara Stevens heard Jimmy's cheery whistle echoing in the hallway long before he strolled into the church office. She joined the congregation and staff in their deep affection and strong respect for Jimmy Perkins. During his first year as the singles pastor he had weathered some heavy storms in a ministry group that had seen its share of struggles, especially in the area of sexual morality. Yet while standing firm in the midst of each squall, he never lost his temper or his tenderness. His outlook remained positive, his smile was infectious, and the people couldn't help but love him.

"Hi, Jimmy!" she called as he approached her office on the way to his own. Barbara was old enough to be his mother, and sometimes she even looked at him as more a son than a pastor. But the age difference never stood in the way of a healthy conversation, and she could use one right now.

He stopped outside her door and with a warm smile answered, "Hi, Barb. How are you today?" From most, the question was merely a token courtesy, but Barb had learned that when Jimmy asked, he asked sincerely. Now, however, the question also seemed seasoned with an empathetic tone.

"I'm doing OK, I guess," she replied. "Pastor Benson surprised me this morning, but I probably should have seen it coming. Things have been strained for a while, and I suppose it was only a matter of time."

Jimmy had gradually shifted inside her office and leaned back against the door jam, casually crossing his right leg over his left. He held his clipboard against his chest with folded arms as he focused his attentive eyes on hers. After an understanding sigh, he added, "Yeah, I never expected that kind of display. Not from him. He has always been so strong."

"Jimmy, why do crises always seem to come in groups?"

"What do you mean?" he answered.

"I just came back from lunch with Liz Thompson—you know, the Governor's secretary. We've been friends for years, and from what she said, everything's crazy over there, too."

"I'm not surprised," he offered. "When I read that article this morning, I was pretty disgusted. If he's guilty, I hope they convict the guy. And it doesn't look good for Gov. Bates either, does it?"

"No, it doesn't," she agreed. "I've had doubts about the governor from the beginning. And, from what Liz has told me, this may be only the surface. It seems that things over there are getting worse all the time."

After a brief but reflective pause, she added, "Jimmy, how do you think God views all of that mess in the Capitol? I mean, of course it's wrong, and God hates sin, but you've just got to wonder how long He will put up with it all before He gets tired of it and deals with the whole lot of them."

"You're right," he responded. "You know, for a long time it never really bothered me. I saw government as one of those 'necessary evils' we have to put up with in a sinful world. When politicians were caught in a lie or even in a crime, I just figured that's the way politicians are and I didn't expect much different. My focus was on 'seeking first the Kingdom of God and His righteousness.' This government is *certainly* not the Kingdom of God, and most politicians know *nothing* of His righteousness, so I never gave it much thought.

"But then Gov. Bates was elected, and I seriously began to wonder. I started studying in Matthew where Jesus called His followers to be 'salt' and 'light' in the world. Of course, the main way we do that is through sharing the gospel and living godly lives. But it seems to me that God expects more. If He hates sin in our government and desires something different, it seems that He also would expect us to take a visible stand against that sin. I personally don't believe He wants us to watch the government disintegrate before our eyes while we sit on the sidelines singing 'Amazing Grace.'"

"OK, but what about Pastor Benson's view on this?" Barbara replied. "Whenever I hear about 'the separation of church and state,' I get nervous and wonder just how far we should go. I know things are bad, but how can I be sure that God *really* wants me to be involved? And does this mean that I have to join some kind of radical, religious political group?"

Just then the receptionist's voice interrupted on Barbara's intercom. "Barb, is Jimmy back there?"

"Yes, he is, Judy."

"Would you please tell him that he's got a call on line 2?"

"I sure will, Judy. Thanks."

"I'll get that in my office," Jimmy said as he flashed his famous smile, "but you hold that thought!"

Barbara Stevens' question may be on the hearts of many believers across the nation. On one hand, we see the immorality in our government and legal system and we're certain that it angers God. From what we saw in the last chapter, the U.S. isn't far from the corruption of Judah during Isaiah's day and it probably wouldn't surprise us if God poured out His wrath on the nation.

At the same time, some of us may be uncomfortable with the thought of being "politically active." For years many of us have observed the clear distinction between the Kingdom of God and all earthly kingdoms. Like Jimmy Perkins, we've devoted ourselves to seeking first His Kingdom, and we've separated that sincere and noble pursuit from involvement in earthly kingdoms. We have genuinely joined our hearts with Paul and are *resolved to know nothing . . . except Jesus Christ and him crucified* (1 Cor. 2:2).

Furthermore, some of us can't relate to those religious political groups. Their motives may be pure, but their activities and agendas strike some as irrelevant to Jesus' primary emphasis on making disciples. We struggle to find strong biblical support (especially in the New Testament) for Christians speaking up and leading out in the civil and political arena. And we cry out for some sense of balance on the whole issue.

Once again, we are drawn back to God's Word through Isaiah. So far we've seen His passionate indictment of both the leaders and the people of Judah, His emotional rejection of their worship, and His clear commands related to the civil arena. But we still haven't dealt with the key question that ties all of these together: *Why* was God so passionate in His expectations of justice, relief for the oppressed, and protection for the defenseless?

What was there about God and these expectations that would lead Him to identify the people of Judah with Sodom and Gomorrah?

Why would failure in these civil expectations result in the absolute rejection of their worship? Why would He label this civil failure evil? What stirred the fire of God's passion as He evaluated Judah's civil status and found them desperately lacking? And does His response have any bearing on us today? The answers, again, are in God's Word. As we consider these answers, we'll be another step closer to answering Barbara Stevens' question, a question shared by so many of us.

GOD'S PASSION

It's obvious that God was fiery in His address to Judah through Isaiah. However, if we go back beyond Isaiah into Judah's history, we see the broad picture behind Judah in Isaiah's day. Here we discover at least two reasons why God would react in such an intense manner.

The Nature of God

The ingredients at work in God's stirring charge related to His own nature.

God Is Just

The Scriptures reveal that God is just in His very being. God's throne is pictured as having justice in its foundation (Ps. 89:14). King David declared that God loves justice (11:7). The Bible also reveals that all justice ultimately flows from God (Deut. 1:17). He is a just God, and any injustice goes against His nature.

Previously, we clarified our understanding of justice by identifying three key principles of justice: moral standards of right and wrong; the separation of financial influence from legal and civil decisions; and due punishment for the guilty. But as we come to know God better, we find that each of these three principles is evident in God's nature.

In our consideration of the first principle (moral standards of right and wrong), we saw an emphasis on fairness, sexual morality, and the value of human life. When we look at God, we find that He is unequivocally fair in all of His dealings with humankind (Job 34:10-13; 40:1-14), He is entirely free from any form of immorality (1 John 1:5), and He personally places the highest value on human life (Gen. 1:26,27; 9:6). So, when one of His people treated another unfairly, or was sexually immoral, or disregarded the value of human life, that person defied the nature of his Creator and Deliverer.

Our study of justice also focused on the separation of gifts and bribes from the legal and civil arena. When we consider the Person of God, we find that He is not partial in any of His dealings and cannot be swayed by gifts or bribes (Deut. 10:17; Rom 2:11). Therefore, the leaders whose decisions were influenced by the lure of personal gain also defied God's nature.

The concept of justice also included God's call to punish those who broke the law. When we examine Moses' marvelous encounter with God on Mt. Sinai, we find God revealing Himself in an unprecedented display of His glory. As He passed before Moses, He identified Himself as compassionate, gracious, slow to anger, abounding in love and faithfulness, and exceedingly forgiving. We would be more comfortable if He had stopped there, but He went on to point out that He is a God who punishes the guilty (Ex. 34:6,7).[1] God's nature requires punishment for lawbreakers, and when the legal system of Judah failed in this area, they defied God's nature.

God had revealed Himself to Judah as a God of true and genuine justice. Furthermore, He expected the people of Judah to exercise

His standards of justice in their civil structure. When they failed to do so, they not only disobeyed God, they also defied His very nature.

God Is Concerned

Not only do we find that God is just, but as we seek to know Him better, we also find that God is particularly concerned about the needs of the helpless. He was very careful to point out His concern and compassion for those who were vulnerable and subject to exploitation. God declared to His people that He personally would defend the defenseless of their day (orphans, widows, and aliens—Deut. 10:18-19). He took a personal interest in those who could not provide for themselves and presented Himself as the loving Protector of those who could not protect themselves (Ps. 146:9). In His love and compassion, God displayed a special concern for those who could be victimized by the ruthless and greedy of the day.

But the people of Judah did not share God's concern. The rich conspired with the courts and civil leaders to confiscate land from the poor. Citizens were not protected from criminals, and the defenseless were helpless under the oppression of the wicked. Not only did they defy God's commands, they totally disregarded His nature that displayed a personal concern for those in need.

God Is Loving

A third element of God's nature at work in this picture is His love. As we mentioned earlier, God revealed Himself to Moses as compassionate, gracious, and abounding in love. In fact, God's concern for justice and for the helpless flow directly out of His love. Scholars point out that the concept of justice in the Old Testament was not merely a set of impersonal codes but was inseparably linked to the concept of relationship. It flowed out of God's relationship with His People and was to guide their relationships with each other.[2]

God's concern was not merely for the maintenance of bureaucratic decrees and ordinances. He didn't give laws to bind and restrict His people so they would be miserable—He was concerned for their safety and well being, and this required the establishment of just laws to govern their relationships with each other.

We can even see God's love at work in some of the various elements of justice. When He insisted on fair business dealings among His people, He knew the potential for ruthless and unscrupulous individuals to take advantage of the unsuspecting. Obviously, because of His love He wants the helpless to be protected.

When God insisted upon sexual morality, He knew the potential for self-gratification to dominate and victimize others, as well as themselves. Because of His love, He wanted to protect them from the painful consequences of unshackled self-gratification, so He instituted laws prohibiting sexual immorality and perversion.

God's love is obvious in His laws protecting human life. His love led Him to institute laws that protected people from violence and murder. This wasn't merely an attempt to preserve a society; it was also a clear demonstration of His love for people.

That love is even pictured in the punishment and discipline He assigns to lawbreakers. As we've seen from Moses' Mt. Sinai encounter with God, His punishment is completely consistent with His love. Other passages equate His discipline with the actions of a loving father who is guiding his child (Prov. 3:12).

Parents who truly love their children can easily relate to this concept. We know that if our children don't have guidelines, they are subject to various dangers. If we don't implement rules that forbid them to play in the busy street, they could be seriously injured or killed. If we don't forbid them to play with matches, they could burn down the house and possibly harm themselves in the process.

Furthermore, if our children aren't disciplined when they disobey our loving restrictions, they won't learn the life-saving and life-giving lesson of obedience. As loving parents, we don't institute rules for the sake of rules but because we love our children and want to protect them. And, we don't discipline because we want to make our children miserable, but because we want the best for them.

And so it was with God. He loved His children, and because of that intense love and compassion, He implemented rules to guide their behavior and to protect them from the potential and fatal dangers surrounding them. But He also showed that He was a loving Father who would discipline their disobedience in order that they might live. God even punished unbelievers as a life-giving lesson for His own children.[3] God's love led Him to punish disobedience.

But during Isaiah's day, Judah's perspective on love had been shaded by greed, lust, and pride. Instead of upholding God's love-driven requirement for punishing disobedience, the people twisted the system to suit their own desires. As they failed to execute fair discipline, they defied God's love.

Judah's attitude and behavior demonstrate they had lost sight of their Father's nature. Their God was a God of justice, protection, and love. But in their selfish preoccupations they had ignored God's desire and defied His very nature. The people of Judah should not have been surprised at God's outrage. In His love He delivered them from slavery, established them in their homeland, provided for their needs, and protected them from foreign armies. In return, they rejected His standards of justice, overlooked the needs of the oppressed, and forsook the needs of the helpless—and as they did, they insulted Him by defying His very nature.

The Nature of God's People

This broader picture helps us to understand and appreciate God's passionate declaration to the people of Judah. However, there was even more at work that further explains the level of God's emotion. It stems from what He expected of His people.

They Were to Be His

When the Israelites were suffering under the bondage of Egyptian slavery, they cried out to God for deliverance. God heard their cries and was intimately concerned for them (Ex. 2:23-25; 3:7). After He commissioned Moses to lead the Israelites, God dramatically and miraculously delivered them from the cruel hand of the Pharaoh.

When God brought them safely into the desert, He established His civil standards for them. But as He prepared them to enter their new land, He also did something entirely new and different. He established a covenant with them in which He would view the people of Israel as "*His* people," and they would view Him as "*their* God" (Ex. 6:2-8; 24:1-9; Deut. 29: 9-15). In this relationship, God would treat them as His own "treasured possessions," pouring His abundant affection, blessings, and love upon them (7:6-9). They in turn were to focus their love and obedient faithfulness upon Him (6:1-9). In this tender relationship, God identified them as His special, *chosen* people. Their deliverance from slavery and very existence as a nation was a demonstration of the special relationship they shared. The nature of the Jewish people was that they had been lovingly chosen.

They Were to Be Like Him

The nature of God's people goes beyond the fact that they were chosen. In God's instruction to His people, He also shared that because of this special relationship, they were to be like Him. God identified Himself as "holy," and so He called His people to be like Him in holiness (Lev. 11:44; 19:2). The Lord identified several areas that He viewed as "detestable," and He expected His chosen ones to view these same things as detestable (Deut. 7:25-26; 18:9-13). God's deliverance and the establishment of this special relationship should have moved God's people to lovingly embrace His concerns and values.

They Were to Reflect Him

Finally, God expected His people to reflect the nature of God to the neighboring nations. When God instructed His people to obey His commands, He told them that the neighboring nations would see their obedience and realize that they belonged to God (Deut. 28:9-10). He also pointed out that if they obeyed and followed Him, other nations would see and respect their wisdom (4:5-8). This pointed directly to God, for it was the Lord who gave them the wise commands to follow. The people's actions were supposed to send a message to the world about God's greatness and love.

On the other hand, if His people chose not to obey Him, He had another message for their neighbors. God was careful throughout His teachings to warn the people of the consequences of disobedience. He told them that if they continued to reject Him and His concerns, their nation would be utterly destroyed (28:15-64). He went on to point out that such an action would send a message to other kingdoms that God punishes disobedience (29:24-28).

Either way, the world was to learn of God's nature by observing His people. If they obeyed, the world would learn of the blessings that God pours out on those who love and follow Him. However, if they insisted on continued rebellion, the nations would learn of God's discipline driven by love.

When Isaiah proclaimed this message to the people of Judah, they had completely rejected God's special, loving relationship with them. While they still belonged to God, they no longer behaved as His chosen ones. They no longer cherished the things that were important to God—instead, they embraced the detestable practices of the Canaanites and worse.

Because of God's loving nature and His loving relationship with Judah His people were supposed to reflect His concern in the areas of justice, relief for the oppressed, and defense for the helpless. When the world looked at their behavior, they should have viewed a living illustration of God's love and compassion in each of these three areas. Instead, neighbors viewed shameless examples of civil scams, legalized oppression, and state-protected murder.

Is there any wonder why God was passionate in His declaration? His people betrayed His love, rejected His concerns, and painted a false picture of God to the world.

In that context we can appreciate the emotion behind His joint indictment in Isaiah 1:10. The leaders of Judah had betrayed God through their warped approach to the civil structure, and the people of Judah betrayed God by allowing the leaders to continue. Both the leaders and the populace were guilty of rejecting God's heart and plan.

This also helps us to understand why God rejected their worship in verses 11-16. For the people of Judah, worship was no longer a sincere demonstration of their love and adoration for God. If they had truly loved and adored God, they would have lovingly and readily embraced and reflected His concerns. Instead, their religious activities merely perpetuated meaningless and offensive ritual, for worship without loving obedience is worthless, and thus, wasted.

This background also explains why God referred to Judah's civil failures as "evil" in verse 16 and why He called them to start "doing right" in verse 17. For God, civil structure was not merely a set of impersonal laws, codes, and ordinances that were necessary to maintain societal order. God's standards of justice flowed out of His nature and reflected His love for people. Therefore, when the leaders and people of the land neglected God's heart in this area, their neglect was evil.

God was indeed passionate in His expectations for the civil government of Judah, and this background helps us to better understand why. But we still haven't addressed Barbara Stevens' question. As we emphasized in the first two chapters, the United States government is *not* the government of Judah, and our nation is *not* considered His chosen people. God did not establish a loving covenant with our nation upon its birth, and He did not establish Himself as our King in a functional theocracy. From this perspective alone, these points don't necessarily apply.

Thus far we've only reviewed the history of God's passion concerning the civil failures of Judah. This alone may not compel born-again believers to agree with Jimmy Perkins and inspire them to address the political fray. However, if we broaden our biblical study, we will find that God indeed has civil expectations of the U.S. and of the believers who live here.

GOD'S ABSOLUTE AUTHORITY

It is true that God was the King over Judah and that their government was directly tied to Him. However, the Bible reveals that some of God's basic expectations for civil government were not restricted to Judah but actually applied to all governments of the worlds. Perhaps they weren't expected for all of the same reasons, but they were, nevertheless, required of all civil structures. Consider the following:

First, as we mentioned earlier, God is the ultimate source of *all* justice (Deut. 1:17; Isa. 40:14). This was significant for Judah, but its truth transcends the civil structure of Judah. Because God is the source of all justice, all civil structures that are founded on a system of justice ultimately must look to Him for the nature of justice.

Second, the Bible teaches throughout that all kings and all kingdoms fall under God's rule and must answer to His absolute authority. No government is exempt. The Scriptures boldly proclaim that all earthly governments exist because of God and are subject to His rule. He is the King of kings and Lord of lords![4]

Third, we find that as the absolute King over every kingdom, God expects earthly kingdoms to follow His standards of justice. He demonstrated that His standards of justice were not restricted to Judah but applied to all kingdoms.[5] God also indicated that He expected all kings, rulers, and princes to follow His standards of justice (Prov. 8:13-16).

God's basic principles of justice were not reserved for the government of Judah but are expected of all earthly governments. This is further demonstrated in the New Testament, where God declares His authority over every government and His expectation of those governments to protect the citizens by punishing criminals (Rom. 13:1-6; 1 Pet. 2:13-14).

The fourth point provides perhaps the most compelling evidence for God's universal expectations of civil justice. The multiple accounts of God's judgment upon nations that defied His standards of justice verify His expectations of these secular governments. Consider the example of the Canaanites. We saw earlier that God warned His people not to follow their examples of sexual perversion and child sacrifice. But the Scriptures go on to declare that the Israelites' possession of Canaan was an act of God's judgment upon the kingdoms of Canaan.[6] Their legalized perversion destroyed families and victimized the helpless. Their child sacrifices were examples of legalized murder, and both of these mocked God's standards of justice. God instituted civil structure to maintain these elements of God's justice, but the Canaanites consistently failed to apply and enforce this structure. Therefore, God pronounced judgment upon them.

We find another example of secular civil injustice in Assyria. Scholars paint a brutal picture of this ruthless kingdom that was notorious for its violence and cruelty.[7] When Jonah proclaimed God's judgment, the king led out in calling for repentance from their violence (Jonah 3:8). But the revival didn't last, and Nahum eventually returned to Assyria with another prophecy against their empire. Here we find evidence of sexual sin and continued brutality (Nah. 3:1-4). As we have seen, these practices are inconsistent with God's civil standards of justice, and God held the civil leaders accountable for these civil and moral failures.

Through the prophet Amos, God condemned several nations who denied His standards of justice. In the first chapter we find at least four examples of nations that were ruthless in their treatment of the helpless.[8] In each of these nations, the respective kings were identified as guilty. The crimes mentioned in each of these cases were committed by the governments of the nations, and the judgments were directly related to their governmental depravity. Each of them violated foundational principles of God's justice, and God promised judgment upon them and their nations for their unjust actions.[9]

God expected these secular governments to maintain His basic moral standards of justice. Furthermore, these examples show that

God held them accountable for these expectations and judged them accordingly.

This clearly demonstrates that God's expectations of justice, relief, and protection were not merely confined to Judah. God is the source of all justice, He has absolute authority over every kingdom, He expects every government to keep His basic standards of justice, and He ultimately judges every government that fails to maintain His basic civil standards. He did not have identical expectations of these governments to those He had for Judah, and His designs for Judah were different than for the secular nations. But He did expect the basic civil standards of justice, relief, and protection—standards that flowed from and reflected His very nature.

And God has not changed. But dare we suggest that God might expect the United States government to operate according to these same basic principles? Does God expect our nation to abide by these same moral civil standards that are rooted in the Person of God? Does He expect the judicial and legislative functions to be free from the influence of gifts and bribes? Does God *really* expect our civil system to punish criminals?

Is God truly concerned about the victims in our society, those who have suffered at the hands of the ruthless? Is He still opposed to a civil structure that not only allows sexual perversion but seems at times to endorse it? And does God's heart cry out for the helpless and defenseless children who are slaughtered daily with no civil structure to protect them? Does He still view these violations as "evil?" Unequivocally, undeniably, and absolutely YES! His nature has not changed, His love continues, these passages apply to our nation, and thus His civil expectations apply to us.

God is still the source of justice, He is still the absolute King over every king and nation, He still expects the nations to abide by His justice, and He still promises judgment to all kings and kingdoms that do not bow down to Him. His nature continues to be reflected in His expectations of civil government, and the U.S. Government is not exempt from those expectations.

Therefore, while we are not a theocracy and those particular elements do not apply to our government, our nation is subject to the civil expectations of God.

GOD'S PRESENT-DAY PEOPLE

But what of our responsibilities as Christians in the civil structure? Does God expect us to play an active role in maintaining His civil standards? It is clear that we are citizens first in God's eternal Kingdom and that our affections and energies belong to that King. Also, the people of Judah were living in "their" land, for God had given it to them as their possession. We, however, do not own the land but are, instead, temporary tenants. Our permanent home with our loving Father still awaits us, and that is the focus of our true longing. But does this precious truth exempt us from embracing and reflecting God's priorities until we get home?

Earlier we considered the account of when God lovingly established the Jewish people as His chosen people. That event was a beautiful picture of God's miraculous delivery from Egyptian slavery followed by a new and very special relationship between them. We also saw that the relationship should have resulted in the people's embracing His priorities and reflecting His loving nature to the world.

Yet as we look to the New Testament we also find the same emphases in the relationship between God and those who have been saved by the sacrifice of Jesus Christ. The New Testament teaches that through the blood of Christ, God delivered us from cruel bondage to sin and established a "new covenant" with us

(Luke 22:20; Rom. 6:15-18). Those who have been miraculously delivered from this slavery to sin are also called "a chosen people, a royal priesthood, a holy nation, a people belonging to God" (1 Pet. 2:9, NIV). Furthermore, in Jesus' Model Prayer, He addressed God as "Our Father in heaven" (Matt. 6:9). This reference to God as the "Father" of Jesus' followers shows that these people had entered into a unique and tender relationship with God. Because of God's incomparable love, the redeemed are a "chosen people" who have been brought into a special, intimate, and loving relationship with the Almighty God of the universe.

Also, in the same way that Judah was to embrace God's priorities, we too are to embrace His priorities. He instructed us to be holy as He is holy (1 Pet. 1:16), and to love each other because He loved us and because He *is* love (1 John 4:7-8). God calls His chosen ones to hate what is evil, cling to what is good (Rom.12:9), and to seek first His Kingdom (Matt. 6:33). God *still* expects His chosen people to share His concerns and to embrace His priorities.

Finally, in addition to our status as His chosen people and our responsibility to embrace His priorities, we also are to reflect His nature to the world around us. When the lost observe us and our behavior, they should see an accurate picture of God's glorious nature (1 Pet. 2:12). When they watch us relate to each other, they should learn of the Lord's love (John 13:34,35; 17:23). When the world views our marriages, they should see a picture of the relationship that exists between Christ and the Church (Eph. 5:22-33). As God's people, our priorities, actions, and affections are to project His nature to the world so that the lost can get a small glimpse of what God is like.

God has indeed delivered us from bitter slavery and brought us into a wonderful and loving relationship with Him. Because of this incomparable love and grace, we should respond by eagerly embracing His concerns and warmly reflecting His nature.

Implications

We've seen that God has absolute authority over all civil governments, including that of the United States. We've also seen that He has basic civil expectations of justice, relief, and protection from all civil governments, including that of the United States. In addition, the study has shown that these civil expectations are not merely codes but a reflection of the very nature of God and His love. Moreover, it is clear that God expects His people to embrace His desires and reflect His nature. Finally, we live in a nation where the leaders are elected by the people to reflect the desires and priorities of the people.

Therefore, if God's heart breaks over our nation's civil immorality, shouldn't tears flow from our eyes? If we care about the things that concern God, shouldn't we be concerned about blatant violations of His most basic civil expectations? Because our government is representative, shouldn't we seek representation of God's concern on moral issues? If we have the legal means and opportunity to reduce, and in some cases eliminate, the most flagrant examples of civil injustice, would God expect us to do any less? And when God's people fail to address these issues, don't we convey a false message to the lost about God and His nature?

God is still concerned about fairness in the business realm. But when we ignore a candidate's past record of business dealings, we fail to share God's priorities and accurately reflect His concerns. The Lord truly mourns for the innocent victims of legalized gambling; yet when we do not oppose gambling at the polls, we neglect His concerns and portray a false image of God.

Our Father is still passionate about the destruction brought through sexual immorality and perversion. But when we fail to call on our elected officials to stand against legalized and state sanctioned immorality and perversion, can we justify our declarations that we follow the Lord?

God's heart still cries out for the helpless and oppressed. In His love, He still holds human life precious and wants it protected. Yet when we elect so-called "pro-choice" candidates (or *allow* their election by not voting!) who perpetuate the legalized slaughter of the helpless, how can we honestly claim to love God?

When we remain silent at the polls or when we don't call our representatives to action in these areas, the watching world could falsely conclude from our actions that God is not *really* concerned about these issues. They then could logically conclude that the vocal minority of politically active Christians don't truly represent God's heart, but are instead "religious right" fringe fanatics who should be dismissed and ignored as such.

CONCLUSION

God cares about the civil immorality that has consumed our nation, and His concern flows out of His love for humankind. He knows that the collapse of His civil standards destroys people. Furthermore, God expects His people to share and reflect His concern, because of love. *Love* should drive God's people in the U.S. to the polls—love for God and love for the people who are destroyed by violations of His civil standards. Of course, the greatest love is shown in sharing the soul-saving truth of Jesus Christ, but God expects us to reflect His love in other ways as well. And for U.S. Christians, an energized and prayerful participation in the civil process is a tangible and essential way to reflect and demonstrate His love.

Barbara Stevens asked Jimmy Perkins about participating in religious political groups. While there are some fine Christian organizations that provide a vital service by tracking and reporting key political candidates, policies, and developments, this study does not imply that Christians should join up. Contrary to what some well-intentioned advocates might think or suggest, a Christian's spiritual maturity is not measured by the level of participation in or support for such groups.

What these passages clearly demonstrate is that each individual Christian in the United States has a moral responsibility to personally embrace God's civil concerns and reflect those concerns to the world. Every U.S. believer has the crucial responsibility to engage the government in a way that reflects God's priorities.

Our civil standards of justice are crumbling around us, and for us, "seeking first His Kingdom" does not negate an active concern for God's civil standards but actually invokes such a concern. Unfortunately, Jimmy Perkins's observation may be painfully accurate. Far too many of us have been content to watch the government disintegrate before us as we stand on the sidelines singing "Amazing Grace." Now is the time for us to embrace God's continued concern for civil immorality and reflect His loving nature to the watching world. To do less would deny His nature and ignore His love.

1. When we combine this passage with Ex. 20:5, we see a picture of the guilty as those who demonstrate their "hate" for God by continuing in disobedience.

2. Herntrich, *Theological Dictionary of the New Testament*, vol. 3, 926.

3. The destruction of Sodom and Gomorrah was not only punishment for their sin, but also an object lesson for Abraham and his descendants—see Gen. 18:16-19; also, Derek Kidner, *Genesis, An Introduction and Commentary*, (Downers Grove: InterVarsity Press, 1967), 132-133; Allen P. Ross, *Creation and Blessing: A Guide to the Study of Genesis*, (Grand Rapids: Baker Book House, 1988), 350.

4. Consider Psalm 2, Proverbs 8:14-16, Daniel 4:19-37, especially verse 25 & 34; John 19:10,11, Romans 13:1-7, Ephesians 1:20-22, Philippians 2:9-11, I Timothy 6:13-15, Revelation 1:5; 17:14 and 19:16. For additional passages showing God's judgment on kings and nations, see Psalm 2:10-12, Ezekiel chapters 26-32 & 38,39, Daniel 5:18-30, Revelation 6:15,16; and 19:17-21.

5. Ez. 5:6,7; also see Herntrich, 932.

6. See Gen. 15:16, Lev. 18:24; Dt. 9:1-6; also see Kidner, 125.

7. James Montgomery Boice, *The Minor Prophets, An Expositional Commentary*, vol. 2, Micah-Malachi, (Grand Rapids: Baker Books, 1986), 381-383.

8. The Arameans 1:3; the Philistines 1:6-9; the Edomites 1: 11,12 and the Ammonites 1:13,14.

9. For additional passages showing God's judgment on secular kings and nations, see Psalm 2:10-12, Ezekiel chapters 26-32 & 38,39, Daniel 5:18-30, Revelation 6:15,16; and 19;17-21. Consider especially Isaiah's prophecy against Babylon for ruthless brutality and oppression in 13:11 and 14:3-6. Also, Habakkuk presents God's judgment on Babylon for greed, extortion, plunder, bloodshed, unjust gain, unpunished crime and sexual immorality (2:5-17).

Chapter 6

CHOOSING DEATH OVER LIFE

Toni Johnston groaned a little as she eased herself into her favorite booth for a brief but much-needed lunch break. Her back and feet had been screaming at her for some rest after a frantic morning and lunch rush at the Golden Dome Café. Carol had called in sick, so Toni and Maggie had scurried to cover all of the tables. Now, after waiting on every pompous dignitary and cocky young political upstart in the city, she could briefly give in to the pleas of her aching body parts. It was her turn to enjoy a roast beef sandwich with chips, a kosher spear, and iced tea before starting the clean up routine for the day.

After four years at the Dome, Toni had settled in here and had no plans to look for another job. Frank, the slightly overweight owner (and cook), had treated her well. When Bobby, her oldest, was hit by a car while riding his bike to school, Frank gave her the week off with pay and even helped with the hospital bills. Maggie, her senior co-worker, tried to look hard and act tough, but deep down she was a warm-hearted friend with a soul as soft as a puppy. Sometimes Toni endured her job, but most times she enjoyed it. She hoped one day to resume her nurse's training, but that would have to wait for now. The child support and alimony had not been enough to make ends meet. That's why she had answered the ad at the Dome in the first place.

It had been four years since the divorce, but she still battled deep bitterness and pain. They had weathered their share of storms, but she never dreamed her husband would abandon her for another woman. He did, however, leaving the two boys with no father and her in a pit of grief and loneliness. She was doing the best she could with them, playing catch from time to time and taking them to an occasional ball game (when Frank gave her tickets). But she knew it wasn't enough. They needed a father—but he was off chasing his dreams and feeding his fantasies. Soon the boys would be teenagers, and then what would she do?

All of these thoughts and more were put on hold as she sat down to eat and browse through the newspaper. As Toni took a bite of her sandwich, she caught the headlines about John Billings's indictment. She had heard the buzz all morning from the customers but hadn't gotten the full story. As she read, she shook her head and thought, *So what's new? I saw this coming last year. And what's the big deal, anyway? Don't people realize that we're talking about politicians here? Besides, he won't be found guilty. He'll get off just like all the others.*

She took another bite and glanced down to the next story. There she found that a tornado had hit a town in a neighboring state during the night, killing thirty people. *Wow,* she thought, *another tornado!*

Scanning over to the left, she sipped her iced tea and caught the update on the Mississippi River floods. The forecasters were expecting even more unseasonable rain and warned that the river might not crest for two more days!

As Toni's gaze shifted to the center of the page, she was surprised to read about a massive earthquake in Mexico. Early reports indicated that the death toll was over 240, and they expected it to rise. The story went on to emphasize concern over new seismic activity in Southern California.

Finishing off her pickle, Toni looked over to the bottom right-hand corner of the page and saw a troubling story about gang violence in the capital. There had been a drive-by shooting that left one boy dead and another in the hospital. As she read, she felt a surge of alarm welling up inside her. If she wasn't careful, Bobby and Carl could become these two boys in just a few years. Toni began to imagine what it would be like, picturing in her mind the phone ringing and her picking it up to hear the horrifying news of her boys. She hit the mental brakes at that point, unwilling to follow through and imagine the dreadful prospects. Then she began to entertain the notion of moving to a smaller town.

"This is too depressing!" she muttered as she flipped to the comics at the back of the paper. "Maybe these will cheer me up." The *Tribune* placed its comics on the inside of the back page, just opposite the editorial page. As Toni turned the page an editorial cartoon caught her eye. There, in the middle of the page, was a caricature of the Capitol building with threatening storm clouds poised ominously overhead. Descending out of the clouds and aimed directly at the Capitol were four distinct lightning bolts, each with a different name written on it.

As Toni looked closer, she realized that the four names were Gov. Bates's cabinet members who had been indicted in the last three years. Over the main doorway of the Capitol was a nameplate that read "Gov. P.J. Bates." An old man with long gray hair and matching beard was walking in front of the steps of the Capitol. He wore a long robe, an even longer face, and carried a sign that read "REPENT! THE END IS NEAR!"

Toni smiled slightly. She figured Bates's time as governor was up and suspected that he should probably listen to the old man. But her smile faded as a sobering thought crept into her mind. With the front-page stories still fresh in her mind, she wondered, *What if the old man's warning isn't just for Bates? What if it goes beyond?*

"Toni, break's over!" Maggie's gruff voice shattered Toni's train of thought and brought her brief lunchtime escape to an abrupt halt. As she stood and reached for her empty plate and glass, her back and feet cried out for mercy once more. Unfortunately, she was forced to ignore their pleas because the folks being seated at the corner booth looked very hungry and impatient.

Does the editorial cartoon in Toni's copy of the *Tribune* have any relevance for us? Could the old man's warning reach beyond this fictitious Capitol to the actual governmental centers of our nation? Is it possible that ominous storm clouds are gathering over our national and state capitals in response to grave injustices fostered by decades of immoral practices and policies from our civil government? What about the connection in Toni's mind between the events on the front page and the prospect of broad judgment? Were her personal struggles shading her perspective, inclining her toward a global paranoia, or could there have actually been a connection between the two?

Perhaps the questions sound dramatic and alarmist, but what if there is a connection? What if we were to experience an increase in natural catastrophes or see our nation deteriorate into social chaos—could these in some way be connected to His judgment?

This catastrophic scenario may seem inconsistent with the image of a God who claims to be loving and merciful, but is that indeed the case? Can God actually love a nation and bring dramatic judgment upon it at the same time? And even if He can, is this something our nation should be concerned about? When we consider our government's defiance of God's standards, the social unrest across the land, and the natural catastrophes in our nation, should we take note of the old man's warning to "REPENT! THE END IS NEAR!"

Let's return to God's Word through Isaiah for our answers. There we find a picture of God's intense love mixed with warnings of sweeping national judgment.

GOD'S WORD

After Isaiah condemned Judah's civil neglect and clearly re-established God's standards for civil morality, he continued by offering the people a choice. In 1:18-20 we are allowed an even closer glimpse at God's heart as Isaiah declared:

> *"Come now, let us reason together," says the LORD. "Though your sins are like scarlet, they shall be as white as snow; though they are red as crimson, they shall be like wool. If you are willing and obedient, you will eat from the best of the land; but if you resist and rebel, you will be devoured by the sword." For the mouth of the LORD has spoken.*

In these two verses we find a dramatic offer from a loving God who had been exceedingly patient with His people. They were guilty of violating God's civil standards, violations He identified as "evil" and "wrong." We've already mentioned that Judah was guilty of other sins that Isaiah addressed in other sections of his book, but in verse 18 God clearly identified these civil violations as "sin." At this point, however, in an astounding demonstration of grace, He offers to cleanse the people from these civil sins.

Yet in addition to His gracious offer God warned of the grave consequences if they refused to turn from their social and civil immorality.

To appreciate the depth of the patience, grace, and mercy demonstrated in this passage, we must first examine the historical backdrop of Judah's civil immorality that led to Isaiah's address. Afterward, we will consider the dynamics at work in God's threat of judgment.

Judah's History of Civil Immorality

At first glance, this passage does not seem to make a point of the Lord's patience with His people. However, when we examine the history of Judah, God's offer to cleanse and bless His people is nothing short of astounding. For seven hundred years God had tolerated their moral lapses; more specifically, He had tolerated repeated instances of their civil immorality. One of the most flagrant violations of God's civil standards was the people's persistent and rebellious disregard for His sexual standards.

God's focus on justice included clear civil standards of "right and wrong." In the context of civil right and wrong, He forbade adultery, incest, homosexuality, and bestiality. Sexual activity was to be restricted to heterosexual marriage. However, the people of Judah knew that these sexual guidelines had been established long before Moses recorded God's laws on Mt. Sinai. They knew that when God created Adam and Eve, His design for them was that their emotional and sexual needs were to be met in a heterosexual relationship, as opposed to "same-sex" relationships or in sexual relationships with animals.[1] If they looked closely, they also could see that God's social and civil design was for these heterosexual relationships to remain monogamous and permanent.[2]

Furthermore, God's people had the clear illustration of Sodom and Gomorrah (Gen. 13:13; 18:16-19:29). From the ancient account, they were aware of the civil and social decline that accompanies the perversion of God's original sexual design.[3] They could see how the dominating lust for self-gratification could deteriorate into homosexuality and then into sex-crazed anarchy.

But from the beginning, God's people rejected His design. They longed instead for the sexual adventure associated with worshiping pagan idols. When the nation was gathered at Sinai, God commanded the people to remain faithful to Him and to their spouses (Ex. 20:1-4,14). Later, while Moses was still with the Lord on Mt. Sinai, the people convinced Moses' brother, Aaron, to build a statue of a bull so they could worship it as a god. The figure most likely represented the Egyptian fertility god, Apis,[4] and the Israelites gladly added sexual "revelry" to their worship celebration.[5]

Years later, the men of the nation were tempted by the women of Moab to join them in worshiping their god, Baal (Num. 25:1-3). Baal was also a fertility god, and the worship activities were dominated by sexual perversion.[6] Once more, the people were happy to join in such worship. Make no mistake—their primary offense was in violating the covenant with God, rejecting Him as their only God—and they were punished for their idolatry (Ex. 24:1-8). However, part of the appeal of idolatry was the wanton sexual activity associated with it, which was also a violation of God's civil and social standards.

Once the Israelites entered the land of Canaan, they continued to ignore God's commands and design. The author of the Book of Judges records no less than six different times when God's people turned from Him to worship Baal, with all of the associated perversion.[7] By the time the account gets to the heroic figure of Samson, we find a national leader with extremely loose sexual standards

(Jud. 16:1-19). Tragically, the Book of Judges ends with the account of an attempted homosexual rape similar to that in Sodom.

This final instance is another example of the cultural, social, and civil decline associated with the perversion of God's sexual design. God's civil standards of sexual behavior, however, were not instituted to frustrate the desires of humanity but to protect humanity from self-destruction As God's people ignored His design, they began the process of cultural, social, and civil self-destruction.

Later, during the reigns of King Saul and King David, there is little or no mention of widespread sexual immorality. But as King Solomon grew old, he began to worship the pagan gods of his wives (1 Kings 11:4-9). The fertility goddess Ashtoreth is listed as one of his favorites. History and archeology reveal that the sexual activities involved with worshiping this goddess were graphic and perverted.[8] Sadly, Solomon lifted these activities to a new place of prominence in the land.

After Solomon's death, his son, Rehoboam, ruled in Jerusalem. At this point, the Scriptures portray the people of Judah as exceptionally immoral. Sites for the perverted worship of Baal and Ashtoreth were established throughout the land, and for the first time male cult prostitutes were allowed to practice in the land (1 Kings 14:22-24). Not only was this immorality allowed in the land, but for the first time it was sanctioned and protected by the government! Although there were brief times of revival in the land when the male prostitutes were removed and the sexual worship centers were destroyed, for the most part the practices continued until Isaiah's day.

As we've mentioned, the primary offense in these activities was the people's unfaithfulness to God. Included in their unfaithfulness, however, was the violation of sexual standards that were designed to preserve the nation. And, as we've seen, the sexual immorality was not confined to pagan worship activities but spread beyond to infect the values and lifestyles of the population.

Throughout, the civil leadership had the responsibility to enforce God's standards and protect the land from self-destruction. Instead, the leaders themselves were too caught up in the immorality to take a stand against it.

Rampant sexual immorality was not the only violation of God's civil design. In chapter 3, we pointed out that God's design for justice included punishment for those who violated the law. However, for generations the civil leadership failed to punish wrongdoers, so the violations increased. Furthermore, not only did the leaders fail to punish these lawbreakers but they also became the chief offenders. When civil leaders establish a history of blatant and consistent violation of the standards they are called to enforce, the civil structure collapses.

In addition to these, for generations the civil system had consistently failed to care for orphans and widows,[9] and the value of human life depreciated through the years.[10] All of these together demonstrate that God's people and their civil leaders had rejected and defied His clear civil expectations not once or twice, not just a few times, not for only a few years, but for *hundreds* of years. These civil standards were from the One who had lovingly delivered them from slavery, given them a beautiful new homeland, and established them as a nation. They certainly deserved whatever punishment God was prepared to deliver.

An Astounding Offer

Despite this history, verse 18 does not begin with the threat of punishment. Instead, after getting the people's attention and reasserting His civil expectations, God does the unexpected. In an astounding display of compassion, mercy, grace, and patience, God offers to cleanse His people from their sin and give them yet *another* chance! The depth of their sin was immeasurable, but He was willing to wash them as white as snow, to make them as if they had never sinned! They stood on the brink of national collapse, but He was willing to restore their national stability and lavish them with rich blessings.

How could anyone ever accuse God of being cruel and hard-hearted? How could we ever doubt the reality of the depths of God's love? Who else in all the universe would ever act or react in such a way? God is indeed a loving God who passionately and deeply cares for His people and who has consistently displayed this love in extra-ordinary ways. In this light we can appreciate Micah's declaration and join him as he proclaims:

Who is a God like you, who pardons sin and forgives the trans-gression of the remnant of His inheritance? You do not stay angry forever but delight to show mercy (Mic. 7:18).

But, God's offer in Isaiah 1:18-20 was conditional. Earlier, in verse 16, God called the people to remove their evil deeds from His sight and to stop doing wrong. The offer to cleanse them from their sin was tied to their willingness to turn from their civil sins and back to God's civil design. In verse 19, God indicated that His offer of national blessing was contingent upon their willingness to obey His commands in the civil arena. God was willing to cleanse and bless them, but first they were expected to keep their part of the original agreement. If they would, they would receive blessing. If not—judgment.

In verse 20, God warned the people that if they continued in their civil rebellion, they would face grave consequences. To fully appreciate this warning, we must consider it also in light of the history of God's warnings to Judah.

A History of Warnings

Isaiah's sober reminder in verse 20 was not new to the people of Judah. About seven hundred years earlier Moses had made the same point to the Jewish nation as the people prepared to enter Canaan. Moses presented God's gracious offer to bless the people beyond their comprehension (Deut. 28:1-13), but he quickly followed with warnings of severe consequences for disobedience (vv. 15-68). Moses declared that the consequences of disobedience would be drought, disease, national defeat at the hands of foreign armies, widespread confusion, civil unrest, flagrant injustices, and national infestation of pestilence that would destroy their crops and cripple the economy.

As God's people entered the land and turned from Him, some of these warnings became reality. As we mentioned earlier, the Book of Judges records several instances where the people turned from God. In each of these He used foreign armies to get their attention and bring them back to Him.[11]

Years later, after Solomon died and his son Rehoboam became king, the people again turned from God (1 Kings 14:21-24). On this occasion God used the Egyptian king to punish them for their unfaithfulness by allowing him to attack Jerusalem and ransack the temple (vv. 25-28).

But God didn't restrict his options for national discipline. The writings of Isaiah and his prophetic contemporaries reveal that God also used natural catastrophes as tools for discipline. They pictured God's judgment in graphic terms of destruction through massive flooding (Isa. 28:17; Hab. 3:8), violent earthquakes (Isa. 2:19-21; Hab. 3:6; Amos 8:8; 5:25; Zech. 14:5) and brutal hail (Isa. 28:17). They also promised severe punishment through relentless rain, destructive windstorms, and raging fires (29:6).

When the people saw the threat from foreign powers, widespread disease, the prospect of economic collapse, civil confusion and unrest, and cataclysmic natural catastrophes, they were to realize that God was bringing judgment upon the land for disobedience.

God left the choice to the people and leaders of Judah. If they were willing to turn from their injustice, God was graciously willing to forgive, cleanse, and bless them. However, if they insisted on rejecting God's standards for justice, if they continued to ignore the oppressed, and if they persisted in denying protection to the helpless, they were to anticipate the wrath of God. God expected His people to reflect Him and His priorities in these areas. He rightly expected them to embrace these standards so others could learn about their God by their behavior. When His people refused to embrace and reflect His loving nature, they shouldn't have been surprised at the consequences.

OUR CURRENT SITUATION

What does all of this have to do with us? God's gracious offer and these warnings were specifically directed toward Judah, and there is no indication that they have any relevance to the civil condition in the United States. Perhaps not, but is God's judgment of civil immorality restricted to the nation of Judah?

Consider the warning of Psalm 2:10-12, where the psalmist declares:

Therefore, you kings, be wise; be warned you rulers of the earth. Serve the LORD with fear and trembling. Kiss the Son lest he be angry and you be destroyed in your way, for His wrath can flare up in a moment.

This clearly presents God's demand for civil authorities to submit to His authority and expectations. It also presents some sobering consequences for rejecting His design. When our civil leaders and standards defy God's design, we are completely subject to the frightening consequences pictured here.

Also, let's consider Isaiah's prediction of future judgment on the earth in chapter 24. Here, he promised that the Lord would *lay waste the earth and devastate it; He will ruin its face and scatter its inhabitants* (v. 1). He continued in verse 3, adding that *the earth will be completely laid waste and totally plundered.*

These are strong words offering some alarming prospects for our entire planet. But why would the Lord bring such devastation upon the earth? Isaiah points out in verse 5 that it is because the people of the earth disobeyed His laws, violated His statutes, and broke His everlasting covenant.

Every civil leader, structure, and institution is subject to these expectations. So when our civil leaders and institutions violate God's design, we are all subject to the national consequences.

Natural Catastrophes

How is God's judgment pictured in these verses? Isaiah went on to describe the destruction that awaits the earth. In verse 4, he presented an image of the earth as "drying up," "withering," and "languishing." He continued in verse 6, describing the earth's inhabitants as being "burned up." Later, in verse 18, he revealed that there would be torrential rains associated with God's judgment. These verses offer images of drought, fire, and unusually heavy rains, which naturally produce flooding.

Perhaps the most alarming element in Isaiah's prediction is his reference to future massive destruction by earthquakes. In verses 18-20, he announced:

The foundations of the earth shake. The earth is broken up, the earth is split asunder, the earth is thoroughly shaken. The earth reels like a drunkard, it sways like a hut in the wind; so heavy is the guilt of its rebellion that it falls—never to rise again.

The prophets spoke of God's judgment being displayed through massive flooding, violent earthquakes, raging fires, relentless rain, brutal hail, and destructive windstorms. We would not presume to conclude that the examples of natural calamities we've seen in our country are necessarily the result of God's judgment on the land. But, in light of our civil immorality, can we rule it out?

Diseases

When God pours out judgment on a nation, it may not be restricted to natural disasters. God warned Israel of rampant disease, social confusion, and civil unrest. Haven't we also seen these in our land? Could something be afoot here that we are missing? Medical authorities warn that certain strains of bacteria are becoming increasingly resistant to antibiotics, resulting in a dramatic increase in life-threatening infections.[12]

Researchers are scrambling to keep up with the spread of certain infections. The Centers for Disease Control & Prevention estimates that the incidence of drug-resistant staph infections in intensive-care units doubled from 1987 to 1997. In England, *The British Medical Journal* reported that eight hundred people died from drug-resistant staph infections in 2002, vs. fifty-one in 1993.[13] A report by the World Health Organization indicates that there are 300,000 new cases of drug-resistant tuberculosis a year in the world, and 79 percent of them are "superstrains," resistant to any three of the four first-line drugs.[14]

Societal Demise

In addition to this ominous threat of destruction by infectious disease, there also appears to be a growing threat of societal collapse within our nation. Bill Bennett paints a bleak picture when he reports that between 1990 and 1999 the rate of sentenced prisoners in the United States increased 60 percent, and that between 1960 and 1999, the rate increased more than 307 percent.[15] Bennett also points out that between 1992 and 1999 there was a 16 percent increase in the percentage of Americans reporting the use of any illegal drug within the past thirty days.[16]

Furthermore, between 1990 and 1998 the percentage of families headed by a single parent increased 13 percent, and between 1960 and 1998, the percentage of single-parent families increased more than 248 percent.[17] The value placed on traditional marriage continues to deteriorate. Between 1990 and 1997 the marriage rate decreased nine percent, and between 1960 and 1997 the rate decreased 33 percent.[18]

The youth of our nation have not been spared from the effects of this societal free fall. Bennett points out that between 1965 and 1998 the juvenile violent crime arrest rate increased 175 percent,[19] and the accounts of aggravated assaults increased 69.7 percent between 1988 and 1998.[20] Statistics also show that between 1990 and 1999 the percentage of all unmarried teenage mothers increased 17 percent, and between 1960 and 1999 the percentage increased more than 430 percent.[21] Bennett goes on to indicate that the percentage of high school seniors using illegal drugs increased 34 percent between 1992 and 1999.[22]

Our nation's knees may be starting to buckle under the burden of disease, social chaos, and civil unrest.

None of us are in a position to definitively conclude that these are evidences of God's judgment on our nation. We cannot presume to know with certainty the mind of God on such issues. We live in a fallen world, and such things happen in a fallen world. But it certainly seems we are poised to receive His judgment.

If so, do we as a nation have any hope? Is it too late to turn back the devastating tide of God's judgment? Perhaps. The evidences we've presented are certainly not very encouraging. It is possible we have passed the point of no return as Manasseh and Judah had (2 Kings 21:1-16; 23:21-27).

Yet perhaps the Lord would have mercy on us. Jonah was sent to Assyria to proclaim God's judgment upon the people. But when the king of Assyria heard Jonah's message, he repented and called upon the whole nation to repent. Consequently, God was merciful and postponed His wrath (Jonah 3:6-10). Micah's prophecy reminds us that God "delights to show mercy" (Mic. 7:18).

If, however, we desire God's mercy on our nation, how could we hope to see it apart from the reversal of our civil immorality? And if we would see this nation turned back from her civil injustices, God's people must be engaged in the process.

This is not to suggest that the primary spiritual need in our nation is governmental in nature. It isn't—it is spiritual and can only be met in the shed blood of Jesus Christ. But the heart of our spiritual need has been demonstrated clearly in and through the political arena. Neither would we suggest that spiritual revival will come through a political or civil "revolution." Someone has said that revival will not arrive on Air Force One. Perhaps not. However, revival is not likely unless God's people reflect His concern for the passengers on board.

CONCLUSION

God has shown extraordinary patience and grace toward our nation, but we dare not presume that these will continue.

We have the biblical mandate to stand and lovingly reflect our Father's compassion for humanity as shown through His civil priorities. The watching world needs to see through our actions that God is concerned about civil right and wrong, punishment for lawbreakers, and laws that are free from financial influence. The world needs to know that God desperately cares for victims of the ruthless and that His heart goes out to those who are helpless and need protection—and He expects His people to actively reflect God's love and care through our words and through our actions.

Even if our stand does not turn the civil tide, we are still called to embrace His concerns and project them to a watching world. As Carl Henry observed:

> "To call the nation to put God first, to strive for societal decency, to display a model of personal godliness and public justice, to return to the house of prayer for spiritual renewal, to reach a confused citizenry with the good news of God's grace, to exude the joy of God in a climate of shameful violence, and to promote truth in the nation's executive offices, justice among judges, integrity among legislators, ... is a service that looks toward the Kingdom of God.

> "Surely 50 million evangelicals will not be held guiltless if they allow the impression to widen that God is indifferent to or is pleased with what is now happening to American society."[23]

---

1. Genesis 2:18-23. See also, Derek Kidner, *Genesis: An Introduction & Commentary*, (Downers Grove: Inter-Varsity Press, 1967), 6; and Allen P. Ross, *Creation & Blessing: A Guide to the Study and Exposition of Genesis*, (Grand Rapids: Baker Book House, 1988), 126.

2. This is not to suggest that God commanded monogamous marriages in a formal, specific directive. He didn't, but His design was obvious and implied (see Kidner, p 66, and Ross, p 127), and virtually every key figure in their history who violated this design met with crisis. Abraham's sexual relationship with Hagar resulted in family strife (Genesis 16:1-15; 21:8-21), as well as national and international strife that has continued until today. Jacob's marriage to both Leah and Rachel (as well as his sexual relationships with their "handmaidens") resulted in jealousy between the wives and between their children (Genesis 29:14-30:24). David's polygamous relationships resulted in family strife that plagued him and his kingdom (2 Samuel 11-19:8). Solomon's notorious polygamous relationships led to his spiritual demise (1 Kings 11:3-

10), and to family strife which ultimately contributed to the split of the kingdom (1 Kings 11:26-12:24.

3. This perversion is illustrated not only in the homosexual presence, but in Lot's willingness to offer his virgin daughters to satisfy the mob, and in his daughters' readiness to have an incestuous sexual encounter with him (19:30-38).

4. J. Alexander Thompson, "Apis," *Zondervan Pictorial Encyclopedia of the Bible,* vol. 1, Merrill C. Tenney, general editor, (Grand Rapids: Zondervan Publishing House, 1980), 200. This action represented a corruption of their worship, for Aaron identified the bull as Jehovah, yet they duplicated the sexual immorality of the Egyptians.

5. The word for "revelry" is used elsewhere as a sexual connotation. Consider Isaac and Rebekah in Gen. 26:8 (see J. Barton Payne, "sahaq" *Theological Wordbook of the Old Testament,* Vol. II, 763). Also, even aside from the Egyptian god Apis, the image of the bull was commonly associated with the notion of fertility. See Arthur E. Cundall, "Baal," *Zondervan Pictorial Encyclopedia of the Bible,* vol. 1, 432. Furthermore, consider the sexual connotations of the Egyptians in Ezekiel 16:26. There were strong sexual overtones in the entire context of this idol.

6. Cundall, p 433; also Bruce K. Waltke, "Baal," *Theological Wordbook of the Old Testament,* vol. 1, 120.

7. Judges 3:7-30; 4:1-5:31; 6:1-8:32; 8:33-12:7; 13:1-16:31.

8. William White, Jr., "Ashtoreth," *Zondervan Pictorial Encyclopedia of the Bible,* vol. 1, 359-361.

9. Consider the example of Ruth who should have had no fear in gleaning grain from the harvest field, but instead risked her safety to do so. See Ruth 2:2,8-10 and comments by Hubbard. p 137-138, 159. Also, consider the plight of the widow in 2 Kings 4:1.

10. Consider the story of the wicked Benjamites in Judges 19:20-30 who wanted to rape the guest, but instead raped his concubine, resulting in her death. An irony here is that the men of the tribe of Benjamin saw nothing wrong with the activity (20:12-15). They were indeed punished for the atrocity, but no mention is made of the host who was willing to sacrifice his own virgin daughter to the mob, or of the Levite who seemed to have no input in the offer of his concubine. This indeed represents a low view of human rights as well as a low view of life (see also Cundall, p. 197).

11. See endnote #7.

12. "Killer Staph Is Hitting The Streets: Drug-defying strains of the bacteria have moved way beyond hospitals," *BusinessWeek* Online, April 12, 2004.

13. Ibid.

14. "Around the Globe, Drug-Resistant TB Is Rampant," *New York Times,* March 16, 2004.

15. William Bennett, *Index of Leading Cultural Indicators 2001,* Empower.Org, 22.

16. Ibid., 29.

17. Ibid., 51.

18. Ibid., 56.

19. Ibid., 17.

20. Ibid., 18.

21. Ibid., 119.

22. Ibid., 134.

23. Carl F.H. Henry, "The Uneasy Conscience of Modern Fundamentalism," *Christian Citizens,* Richard D. Land and Louis A. Moore editors (Broadman and Holman Publishers, Nashville: 1994), 60.

Chapter 7

MORE PRESSING ISSUES

The Reverend Lawrence P. Benson dragged himself into his office as if he were lugging the entire fifteen-hundred seat sanctuary on his back. He picked up his mail from Barbara's desk and attempted a cheerful greeting for his faithful secretary. His attempt, however, fell short, and as he passed through the door into his study, he mused to himself that the failure seemed characteristic of his life right now.

His emotional display in front of the entire staff that morning had left him embarrassed and uncomfortable as he faced them. He hadn't planned to unload, but after he opened up about the apparent stalemate at the church, he couldn't help it. Now he had to project the image that everything was OK and that his staff had no reason to worry about him.

He certainly didn't feel like coming back to the office after lunch, and he wouldn't have if he could have cancelled his three o'clock counseling appointment. This one could not be cancelled—it was with Gerald and Denise Collins. Gerald was one of the trustees, and he might not take it well if the pastor cancelled for no apparent reason. Besides, it wouldn't look good.

Gerald and Denise were coming to their pastor in a last ditch effort to save their marriage. Of course, the congregation and the other trustees never would have guessed there was a problem. They appeared to be the perfect couple, the "Barbie and Ken" of Capital First Baptist. They always smiled, always laughed, always dressed well, always held hands during the worship service, and always looked so happy.

As a family, they seemed to have everything. Gerald's new Mercedes illustrated his success as an investment broker. After eleven years in the industry, he had worked his way up the ladder and now owned his own very lucrative firm. When their second child was a year old, Denise got her realtor's license and quickly established herself as a savvy businesswoman. She had opened her own office four years earlier, and now she had six very productive realtors working for her.

Those who worked at the church day-care center couldn't help but envy Denise when she pulled up in her BMW each night at 6:30 to pick up the kids. As they watched her leave for home (some speculated that their house cost *at least* $750,000!), they wondered what it would be like to have it so good. Only a few in the church could identify with their financial status, but most deeply longed for it.

Pastor Benson was somewhat surprised when they first approached him. But as he spent time with them, he saw that they had done an excellent job of acting. Their initial complaints were typical of most marriage counseling sessions. Denise said that Gerald was never home. When he was home, he never wanted to talk and was only interested in her for one thing. Gerald said that she made too many demands on him and was never interested in making love. Furthermore, the kids were out of control and were driving them both crazy.

After a couple of sessions, Pastor Benson realized that priorities and time were serious problems for them. The only time they were consistently together as a family during the week was when they sat next to each other on Sunday mornings. Every day Gerald left early and came home late. Two nights a week he played tennis, usually with clients to firm up their business relationship. On Saturday he typically played golf with friends or potential clients. Denise had Pilates class three nights a week; their oldest child, Ricky, had karate class three nights a week; and their daughter, Chelsea, had ballet twice a week. In addition to these were all of the church activities during the week.

However, after a private phone conversation with Denise, Pastor Benson found that there was an even deeper problem. She revealed that for the last few years, Gerald had been buying *Playboy* from time to time. He said that he was more interested in the articles than the pictures and told her she had nothing to worry about. Then, over the last year or so, he had started watching an occasional "soft porn" movie on cable. A few months ago he brought home two "adult" videos, explaining that they might help their "problem."

Denise was hesitant to share this with Pastor Benson because of Gerald's position at the church, but she admitted that it had gradually done something to her. At first there was a certain dark excitement about it all, but now it was as if something had died inside. She was sick of the whole ugly mess and didn't know if she could ever rekindle those old, good feelings again.

As a result, Gerald and Denise had been fighting consistently for several months and had even talked about divorce. They both knew that breaking up would be hard on the kids, and a divorce right now would also hurt their businesses. Besides, they had both grown up in church and knew that the Bible taught against divorce. So they agreed to try counseling. At first Gerald was hesitant to go to the pastor. He wasn't comfortable with the prospect of his pastor knowing their family secrets. It was tough on his pride, but finally, after more cruel words and bitter disputes, Gerald agreed.

Pastor Benson knew that he could give them some suggestions that might help for a while, but these wouldn't solve their real problems. Also, the problem stretched beyond the struggles in Gerald and Denise's relationship. This whole situation placed the pastor in a very awkward and delicate position. Gerald was not only a trustee, but the couple were among the most generous and faithful givers in the church. If he talked to Gerald about reprioritizing his time, and he followed the advice, their income might drop and their giving decrease. On the other hand, Gerald might get upset and stop giving altogether. Furthermore, Benson was certain that Gerald would become livid if he raised the issue of the magazines and videos.

Benson's dilemma stemmed from the church budget. Four years ago the church built a new, luxurious sanctuary. Because of the lavish design and all the "extras," the church went into deep debt to finance the construction. They weren't afraid of the debt, because they had faith that a new sanctuary would attract more folks, attendance would grow, giving would increase, and they could pay off the mortgage. Gerald and a couple of the other trustees were on the building committee, and they pledged large annual amounts to demonstrate support and confidence. Their example inspired other members to do the same.

Unfortunately, they took a five-year mortgage with a balloon payment at the end of the fifth year. Pastor Benson was confident that they would be able to pay it off at that time and encouraged the congregation to step out in faith. That huge payment was now only thirteen months away, and the increases and pledges had not come as expected. If Gerald's giving decreased, the church couldn't meet their general budget expenses, much less the building budget. And if they didn't pay off that balloon payment, there would be some *very* unhappy members in the church. Benson would then have a whole new set of problems to deal with.

Pastor Benson had to be very careful with how he handled this situation. Gerald was a close friend to two of the other trustees who held similar business priorities. Together, their pledges totaled about 25 percent of the building fund, and they were very influential with other big givers in the church. If they all got upset with the pastor, it could spell financial disaster for the whole church. Benson wasn't about to face that with his members, much less face his pastoral peers who had watched their progress closely.

At the same time he knew that Gerald had to deal with this sexual sin and that both Gerald and Denise were too caught up in their idolatrous pursuit of financial freedom. If these issues weren't addressed, the family was headed for certain disaster. Furthermore, the pastor realized that Gerald's problem with pornography should probably disqualify him from serving as a trustee. But if he were disqualified, how many other leaders would also have to step down? Then what would happen to the budget?

All of this added to the weight on his pastoral shoulders as he slumped into the chair behind his desk. How was he going to deal with them when they came in today? Perhaps he should refer them to Herb Walkens, with the Capital Christian Counseling Center. Herb had helped a lot of families get back on track, and maybe he could help the Collins family. That way the weight of the responsibility would shift off of his shoulders and onto Herb's. *Besides*, he thought, *that's why he gets paid "the big bucks." And if Gerald gets mad at Herb, so what?*

Just then, Barb interrupted his thought. "Pastor, Joe Williams from CAP is on line three. Are you able to take his call right now?"

CAP (the Coalition Against Pornography) was collecting signatures on a petition to close down the adult bookstore that had opened two blocks from the high school. Joe Williams had contacted Pastor Benson before to see if anyone from the church might coordinate a petition drive within the congregation. Benson was skeptical because most of the members just didn't have the time or energy for this kind of thing. At the same time, he didn't want to be labeled as uncooperative in such an effort.

"Thank him for calling, but tell him that I'm not able to talk right now. Also, tell him that I've decided to have Jimmy Perkins handle this issue, and that he should speak with him."

Jimmy seems suited for this kind of thing, he thought to himself. *Besides, I've got my hands full with more pressing issues right now.*

"More pressing issues." Sounds familiar, doesn't it? The demands and pressures of life seem to be on the increase, and discretionary time is definitely on the decrease. One of the results is that we just don't have the time to get involved in some very worthy causes. Of course it is unthinkable for an adult bookstore to open within two blocks of the high school, but who has the time to get involved? There's no debate over the need; the real issue at hand is *time*.

The nature of our jobs and the high cost of living seemingly demand that we devote fifty to sixty hours a week (and sometimes more) to our careers. It's hard enough for some of us to carve out quality time for our children and spouses, much less take the time to help carry the most recent civil or social torch. Add to that the pastor's call for more participation in the ministries of the church. If we're going to be faithful to the Lord's work, we need to be there three and sometimes four times a week. And to make matters worse, daily we must battle the intense and exhausting pressures of living in a morally corrupt world that is desperately trying to pull us down with it. You can't even turn on the TV without being blitzed with some kind of temptation!

How can we answer all of these demands and still have the time (not to mention the energy!) to make a dent in the social ills surrounding us? Yes, the civil sins of our nation are serious and may even prove deadly for the country, but isn't our first responsibility to our families and church? And if these dominate our time and energy, wouldn't we be cheating our families and God to get involved in another social crusade? Besides, Christians aren't permanent residents on this planet, only visitors. Our global ship is truly sinking, so why should we devote precious time and energy to polishing its brass? We've got our hands full with matters that just take a higher priority.

Or so it would seem. If these statements are consistent with God's desire and His design for His people, then these conclusions may be valid. If Pastor Benson, Gerald and Denise Collins, and the rest of the folks at Capital First Baptist reflect the heart of God for His people and His plan, then we all would be justified in overlooking the civil immoralities we've addressed so far in order to focus on higher priorities. But if they don't, we may have found an underlying root for our broad neglect in the civil arena. We've demonstrated that God expects us to reflect Him and His civil priorities in our civil setting and that failure to do so is sin. So why is it that more Christians have not been involved? Perhaps part of the answer is that we've just not realized that this is God's concern for His people. Some of us may not have known that this is important to the Lord. If this is truly the case, then after coming to grips with God's Word, these folks will be anxious to address civil immorality because they embrace God's priorities and want to reflect these to the world.

Perhaps others feel that it is disrespectful to challenge the decisions of our civil leaders. If so, then a gentle reminder of our democratic heritage and structure would remove this barrier.

Perhaps still others have believed the recent (and inaccurate) emphasis on the separation of church and state that challenges Christians to keep their moral convictions to themselves. For these folks, this study, combined with an understanding of the nature of our democratic republic, should eliminate all hesitance.

However, for most of us, these may not apply. What if there is a deeper problem that hinders our participation and influence in the civil arena? What if we have ceased to care about this arena because of a root problem that produces more pressing issues? Suppose our real problem is not as much insufficient knowledge as it is misplaced affection?

Let's return one last time to our beloved brother, Isaiah, and consider his closing words to his first chapter. Here we get a glimpse of Judah's sins that led to their civil immorality. As we read Judah's story we will discover principles that will help twenty-first century Christians in the U.S. deal with issues that hinder our civil involvement.

GOD'S WORD

So far in our study of Isaiah's first chapter, we've seen an unusual combination of fiery condemnation and tender mercy. In the closing verses of chapter 1, Isaiah continued his condemnation of civil sin. In verse 21, he declared:

See how the faithful city has become a harlot! She once was full of justice; righteousness used to dwell in her—but now murderers!

He went on to proclaim in verse 23:

> *Your rulers are rebels, companions of thieves; they all love bribes*
> *and chase after gifts. They do not defend the cause of the father-*
> *less; the widow's case does not come before them.*

Isaiah then continued in verses 24-31 to give additional warnings of future judgment. But as we reflect on these final verses, a logical question for the reader is "Why?" Why would God's people consistently neglect areas that were so important to their God? Surely they knew that these matters were high priorities to the God who delivered them from slavery and established them as a nation. Why, then, would they become so cold to these concerns and threaten their national security with prolonged neglect and disobedience? Why would they reject the standards of the One who loved them and who had repeatedly demonstrated that He was worthy of their love.

This final section shows that the people didn't suffer from a lack of knowledge but from misplaced affections. In the closing portion of Isaiah 1 we find references to Judah's pursuits and preoccupations in four areas—areas that distracted them from their focus on God. These references show that rather than embracing God's priorities and reflecting them to the watching world, they had embraced their own priorities and reflected their sinful pursuits to the world. As they pursued these priorities, by default they allowed civil sins to take root, grow, and gradually destroy their society.

We'll consider each of these areas and then compare the pursuits of ancient Judah with those of American Christians.

The Pursuit of Material Pleasures

As Isaiah chastised the leaders and people of Judah in verses 21-23, he interjected a statement in verse 22 that identifies one element of Judah's misdirected affections and pursuits. Here he stated: *Your silver has become dross.* This brief reference to materialistic greed reflects and addresses the context of Judah at the time. In Chapter 2, Isaiah further addressed the condition when he observed in verse 7: *Their land is full of gold; there is no end to their treasure.*

Still, we can't fully grasp the depths of Judah's sinful preoccupation with materialistic pleasure until we again consider the historical setting of Isaiah's day. Judah's beginnings were shaky at best. After Solomon died, the kingdom of Israel divided into two separate kingdoms: Israel to the north and Judah to the south. Immediately, Judah was rocked with moral and international instability (1 Kings 12; 14:21-31). For about 150 years she fluctuated morally and struggled internally and internationally.

However, during the fifty years prior to Isaiah's ministry, both Judah and Israel experienced a period of peace and prosperity. Judah's King Uzziah implemented military policies that strengthened Judah's borders and secured her against international threat (2 Chron. 26:6-9,11-15). During this time of peace, Uzziah also implemented strategic policies that bolstered national production and fostered lucrative international trade (vv. 26:8,10).[1]

The result was a time of unparalleled peace and personal prosperity for most of Judah's people. A nation that had experienced national and economic instability was suddenly bathed in abundance and tranquility. But, as they tasted the fruit of prosperity, they developed an insatiable appetite for more. Scholars tell us that the people of Judah shifted their focus from God's gracious and abundant provision to their own yearning for the delights of luxury. [2]

Previously we discussed the greed of wealthy landowners and God's condemnation of their ruthlessness. We also discussed the greed of Judah's leaders. But history reveals that the pursuit of materialistic pleasure was not restricted to the leaders.[3] The people had tasted the "finer" things in life and wanted more. The leaders merely reflected the mind-set of the people. Together they engaged in a constant pursuit of "just a little bit more." Collectively they had succumbed to the subtle seductions of luxury.

It was difficult for people who were caught up in the pursuit of luxury to challenge their leaders who were engaged in the same pursuit. It was also difficult for people to pay attention to their leaders' activities when they themselves were consumed by their own materialistic pursuits. Their focus on wealth and possessions seemed to foster a cloud of apathy over civil matters. They no longer cared, for they had more pressing issues at hand.

The people's neglect of God's civil design was in itself sin, but the seed of that sin grew in the ungodly greenhouse of greed.

The Pursuit of Sensual Pleasures

The source of the people's apathy extended beyond materialism. After Isaiah raised the issue in 1:22, he also stated: *your choice wine is diluted with water.* This statement raises the issue of Judah's preoccupation with the pleasures of the senses. One of those sensual pleasures was drunkenness. The people of Judah had a reputation for abusing alcohol and relishing the party atmosphere associated with drunkenness. Later Isaiah chastised the people of Judah for pursuing drunkenness, declaring: *Woe to those who rise early in the morning to run after their drinks, who stay up late at night til they are inflamed with wine* (5:11).

It seems the people of Judah even magnified drunkenness into a form of competition. Isaiah warned: *Woe to those who are heroes at drinking wine and champions at mixing drinks"* (vv. 22).

These demonstrate that the people had shifted their focus from God's priorities to the priority of "feeling good." But their preoccupation with feeling good did not restrict them to merely getting drunk. They also sought sensual pleasures through sexual immorality.

Toward the end of his first chapter, Isaiah alludes to this when he addresses the people's idolatrous "delight." We emphasized earlier that much of the idolatry in Isaiah's day involved the worship of pagan fertility gods and goddesses—bizarre worship practices that included gross sexual immorality. It's not difficult to see why some would be drawn to this type of worship!

Not only did the people violate God's direct commands, but it also became an obsession with many. Isaiah's contemporary, Micah, accused the people of following the pattern set by the former Israeli kings, Omri and Ahab (6:16). We're told that these two kings were the most vile and corrupt in the history leading up to the time of Isaiah (1 Kings 16:25,29-33). They were very active in the worship of Baal and Ashtoreth, and they clearly projected the priority of self-gratification. Micah warned that God's people were living out that same priority.

Their pursuit of sensual pleasures became blinders that kept them from focusing on God's priorities. They liked feeling good, and after they tasted the fruit of self-gratification, they became "hooked."

Again, since the people of Judah were absorbed in pursuing sensual pleasures, it would have been difficult for them to have addressed similar sins in the civil government. If the law called for the punishment of sexual immorality, it would have been inconsistent for sexually immoral citizens to have called for the enforcement of that law. Also, those caught up in the pursuit of sensual pleasure probably wouldn't have been concerned about many civil issues unless those issues threatened their own pleasure. They didn't have time to be bothered.

Once more, their civil neglect was indeed sin, but it was cultivated in the fertile soil of sensual self-gratification.

Pride in Accomplishments

Judah was not only preoccupied with materialistic and sensual pleasure, but as we come to the end of Isaiah's opening chapter, we find that Judah struggled in a third area—that of national and individual pride over their accomplishments. In verse 31, Isaiah warned: *The mighty man will become tinder and his work a spark; both will burn together, with no one to quench the fire.*

The people of Judah had become consumed with pride, and Isaiah cautioned them repeatedly about the long-term consequences. He warned them that if they continued, God would humble them in dramatic and painful ways (2:9,11-15; 3:16-23; 5:15,21).

How did they get to this point? What would lead the people of Judah to such unjustified and irrational conclusions? Didn't they see their disobedience? Couldn't they grasp the fact that their ongoing sin overruled any potential cause for pride? The answer is found once again in their history.

As Moses was preparing God's people to enter the promised land, he warned them to beware of the potential for pride. In Deuteronomy 8:10-18, he specifically warned the people not to forget that God was the One who ultimately was the source of all of their blessings. Moses cautioned them that if they weren't careful, after they experienced the blessings of prosperity, they would forget that these came from God. He specifically warned them in verse 17 of the temptation to conclude: *My power and strength of my hands have produced this wealth for me.* He went on in verse 18 to encourage them to:

Remember the Lord your God, for it is He who gives you the ability to produce wealth.

These verses demonstrate that God's concern was not over receiving wealth but about the danger of their losing sight of the source of their wealth. This myopia became reality in the days of King Uzziah when the nation experienced unparalleled prosperity under his rule. The economy not only stabilized, but it grew at an incredible rate. There is no indication that God opposed this prosperity. In fact, it is consistent with all of His earlier promises to bless them if they obeyed (Deut. 8:18; 28:1-14).

After his successful and productive reign, Uzziah unfortunately led the way down the destructive path of pride. The Bible reveals that after he had accomplished so many positive things, he lost sight of the One who was the ultimate cause of his success and credited himself with the accomplishments (2 Chron. 26:16). The nation followed, placing unwarranted pride in their military strengths and economic accomplishments (Isa. 2:7; 3:35). The nation was suffering under the terminal miscalculation that they were somehow responsible for the national security and economic boom of the past generation. They were proud of their national accomplishments, and as they lost sight of the true source, they severed themselves from that source.

Not only did the nation suffer from a national arrogance, they suffered from individual arrogance as well. There were those who took special pride in their own individual accomplishments, failing to recognize God as the One who gave them the ability to work and produce (1:31). This arrogance was demonstrated in the heavy emphasis on dressing to reflect one's status. Isaiah warned the women of Judah who were "haughty," those who flaunted their wealth through jewelry, clothing, hairstyles, and perfumes, that they faced the potential of God's humiliating judgment (3:16-24).

When pride invades the hearts of a nation and its people, it's difficult to admit shortcomings and inadequacies. If a nation is caught up in its own accomplishments, it's a short step to the conclusion that there may be no civil shortfalls. Furthermore, when an individual is caught up in the blinding light of personal accomplishment (or the pursuit of that accomplishment), it's easy to rest in that aura and fail to see the larger civil picture.

So it was with Judah. The people's neglect of God's civil priorities was most certainly sin. But the sin was allowed to germinate, grow, and bear fruit through the husbandry of national and individual pride.

Idolatry

Judah's fourth vice is related to the first three, but it also included a bitter insult against God. Isaiah alluded to Judah's practice of idolatry in 1:29, but he elaborated in chapter 2. In verse 8, he indicated that the land was full of idols. This was a flagrant violation of God's command at Mt. Sinai. When God delivered His people from Egypt, He commanded that they were to have no other gods and that idol worship was forbidden (Ex. 2:1-6). Later He emphasized that they were to recognize God as their Deliverer and Sustainer and were to direct all of their affection and worship toward Him (Deut. 6:1-12).

Sadly, Judah abandoned its love for God and dependence upon Him and redirected these toward the local idols. Worshiping the Canaanite gods and goddesses embodied three vices: materialism, lust, and pride. The wealthiest used gold and silver for their "designer" idols (Isa. 2:20; 40:19; 46:6). Their depraved lusts were satisfied through the fertility rites of the Canaanite gods. The people took pride in the gods and goddesses they produced with their own hands (Isa. 2:8-22).[4] Pagan idols represented the human tendency to focus affections on these vices and then magnify them to the level of deity.

However, the problem extended beyond misplaced and corrupt affections. When the people of Judah worshiped the various pagan gods, they demonstrated that they trusted the Canaanite deities for their security and stability. The gods of the land were thought to be the source of rain, fruitful crops, healthy reproduction, and protection against invading forces.[5] In other words, they looked to the gods for national stability and security.

This was outrageous! It was the consumate offense to God. He had emphasized repeatedly throughout the history of Judah that these kinds of blessings came from one, and only one, source— God Himself. For His people to seek peace and provision from idols formed and crafted by their own hands, instead of from the One who had delivered and sustained them, was not only ludicrous but the definitive insult. God had earned His people's love and trust, but they haphazardly laid these at the feet of undeserving pagan idols.

Their civil neglect was indeed sin, but it blossomed in the garden of idolatry.

Together, Judah's pursuit of material pleasures, sensual pleasures, pride over accomplishments, and idol worship provided the opportunity for civil immorality to take root and grow to lethal levels. Again, the civil sins were serious in and of themselves. God called the people of Judah to repent of these sins and return to His loving design for the civil structure. But these civil sins did not breed in a vacuum. They unfolded as God's people became preoccupied with "more pressing issues."

A Clerical Void

There is a tragic footnote to this discussion. We would expect that the priests and prophets of this period would have joined Isaiah in his rebuke. Instead, they were among those who needed to be chastised. Micah's prophesy reveals that many (if not most) of the priests were afflicted with some of the same misplaced affections.

These religious leaders should have warned the people of the dangers of prioritizing sensual pleasures. Instead, they merrily led the people down the path of decadence. They themselves sought to satisfy their own sensual desires, ignoring God's commands and priorities (Isa. 28:7f; Mic. 2:11).

But their lusts were not only in sensual areas. Micah also records that those who were to guide the people of God instead were preoccupied with their own materialistic goals. We are told that they would structure their ministry and messages according to financial influence (Mic. 3:5,11). If the price was right, the ministry and message were right. If the compensation was inadequate, the ministry and word were structured accordingly. To make matters worse, they did it all in the name of the Lord, under the false assumption that God was with them and would bless their efforts (v. 3:15). They too enjoyed the "good life" and were drawn in by the seductions of materialism.

The clergy of the day had too much going on in their lives to recognize and address civil immorality. Their pursuits (in the name of the Lord) kept them busy, and they could not be distracted. And if they had noticed the civil sin, they were in no position to address the debauchery and greed of the leaders, for they themselves were deeply bound by the same sin.

TWENTY-FIRST CENTURY U.S. CHRISTIANITY

What about today? Are there significant parallels between God's people then and His redeemed ones today? Have we also fallen into those snares of materialism, sensual gratification, pride, and idolatry? If so, have they distracted us from God's civil priorities and from reflecting those priorities to the world? Let's consider each of these separately and see how we compare. First, the issue of materialism.

The Pursuit of Material Pleasures

By international comparison, U.S. citizens have a great deal of discretionary funds. However, as with Judah, having money isn't the problem—it's our attitude toward longing for more that becomes a problem. The evidence shows that we have an insatiable appetite for more, which often takes us beyond our means. According to the Federal Reserve, by January 2004 America's consumer debt had topped $2 trillion for the first time.[7] Debt experts say this demonstrates "an alarming surge" in recent years, for that figure marks a doubling of America's consumer debt in less than 10 years! The average American carries a consumer debt of about $13,000 on items other than a home mortgage.[8] Even more startling is that in 2003 filings for personal bankruptcies reached an all-time high of 1.6 million.[9] This is more than three times the number of filings fifteen years ago![10] The people of the United States have apparently been sucked into a materialistic free fall.

But how have God's people fared? Are Gerald and Denise Collins and the rest at Capital First Baptist the exception to the rule? Or are the Christians of this nation also giving in to the lure of "just a little bit more?" It seems so.

The records show that on average over the last thirty years giving to local churches has consistently decreased, and it doesn't appear to be from a decrease in personal income.[11] The average church member last year gave only $20 to foreign missions.[12] And while the average consumer debt was at $13,000, one church survey of 753 families showed the average consumer debt to be $15,000![13] Finally, while the average U.S. citizen gave 1.7 percent of their income to charitable causes, the average Christian only gave 2.5 percent, which is less than a one percent difference![14] One prominent financial counselor said that he has observed very little difference between Christians and non-Christians when it comes to financial priorities.[15]

Generally, God's people in the twenty-first-century United States appear to have adopted the materialistic values of our unsaved neighbors. Even more alarming, we are dangerously close to the mind-set of God's people in Judah (if we have not caught up to, or even passed them!). Again, God has not opposed wealth and prosperity among His people. Indeed, it seems that He has blessed some of His children financially so that they can help finance His Kingdom causes.

Unfortunately, too many of us have forgotten Paul's example when he declared that he had *learned the secret of being content in any and every situation, whether well fed or hungry, whether living in plenty or in want* (Phil. 4:12). Instead, we face the very real prospect of being consumed and driven by the sometimes-subtle yearning for "just a little more" comfort.

This is not to suggest that every home where both parents are employed is worshiping the gods of material pleasure. Sometimes economic circumstances require long, hard hours in the workplace. There may be times when providing the basic necessities of life demands a heavy workload. And this is not to suggest that having newer and nicer things is necessarily wrong.

But when God's children order their careers, schedules, lifestyles, and families according to the materialistic standards of this world, they are dangerously close to Judah's mind-set. When we no longer are content with our homes, provisions, and transportation (of which even the most modest exceed the dreams of most in the world!), and when we structure our lives around the pursuit of larger homes, nicer provisions, and more lavish automobiles, we have fallen prey to the lethal seductions of luxury. When we do, we lose sight of God's civil passions—because our lives are caught up with more pressing issues.

The Pursuit of Sensual Pleasure

There's hardly any need to review the national obsession with sensual pleasures. While drug abuse may have decreased somewhat over the last twenty-five years, the number of abusers and addicts remains alarmingly high.[16] Producers of strong liquor seem to be flourishing from robust sales.[17] Pornography continues to maintain a death grip on our nation—one report indicates that there has been an 1800 percent growth in the last five years.[18] Our nation's sexual standards have plummeted over the last forty years.[19]

But how are Christians doing in this area? Have we resisted the temptation to indulge and enjoy? Is the example of Gerald Collins an exception to whom most Christian men cannot relate? Let's consider some additional numbers. The study done in the 90s entitled "Sex in America: A Definitive Survey" provided some alarming statistics. It revealed that only half of those surveyed who considered themselves "conservative Protestants" thought that sexual activity should be confined to a monogamous, heterosexual marriage relationship.[20]

Furthermore, only 70 percent of conservative Protestants claimed to have had only one sexual mate in the prior year, while 17 percent admitted to multiple partners.[21] More recently, 50 percent of the men surveyed at a Promise Keepers event admitted to viewing porn within a week of attending the event.[22] And 34 percent of the readers of the *Today's Christian Woman* online newsletter admitted to intentionally accessing Internet porn in a recent poll.[23]

God's people in the U.S. are plagued by the same vices as those in ancient Judah. We are in danger of being consumed by the lust for sensual gratification while losing sight of God's clear commands in this area. Again, we don't look much different than our unsaved neighbors. And it's difficult to become emotionally charged over clear examples of civil immorality when we are losing our own personal battles with sensual gratification.

Pride Over Accomplishments

Of the three vices we've examined, this is the most difficult to measure. Pride over accomplishments is a matter of the heart; and while its presence may be detected, it is not easy to quantify or gather data on the matter. Pride concerning individual accomplishments, whether in the secular realm or in the church, can be far more subtle than the other vices.

This is not to suggest that God has nothing to say to us on the issue. The apostle John warned us to not to boast over what one has or does (1 John 2:15,16). Paul reminds us that God has chosen to work through lowly and unimpressive people so that no one could boast before Him (1 Cor. 1:26-29). Paul also asserts that we have no reason to boast over our accomplishments, for anything good that we have has come ultimately from God and not from ourselves (4:7). Finally, Paul declares that our salvation is not the result of our impressive efforts. Instead, it comes as a gift from God by grace and through faith "so that no one can boast" (Eph. 2:8).

Each of us must individually determine how much emphasis we place on personal accomplishment and status. It would serve us well to ask ourselves if we are concerned about people's opinions of our employment or of our financial status or of the vehicle we drive. Are we quick to inform others of how our business is doing, or of position in the company, or of responsibilities in the community, or of the neighborhood in which we live? Do we find satisfaction in wearing clothes that openly display a certain standard of living? Do we enjoy the fact that we are members of an exclusive club, society, or fraternity? Do we find ourselves trying to keep up with the Joneses?

Is there a certain fulfillment in having attained a higher level of training in my field so that the lay person depends on my expertise (whether my field is law, medicine, business, theology, or auto repair)? Are my diplomas, degrees, and awards boldly and strategically displayed for all to notice? Do I secretly long for approval and recognition from my peers concerning specific accomplishments in my field?

What about in the church? Is it important that others know how long I have been a member or which positions of leadership I hold? Do I want my brothers and sisters to realize how often I am at the church, or how many visitors I have brought? Is it important that they see me put my offering in the plate as it passes? Am I quick to point out how God has blessed my faithful giving? Do others need to know how long I've been a believer and how well I know the Scriptures? Is it important to me that they know the temptations I have faced and conquered? Is it crucial that others know how often and how long my quiet times are? Do they really need to know what verses I have memorized this week?

Do we want the furnishings of our church sanctuary to consist of lavish accommodations that reflect the financial success of the members? Do we want our Christian brothers and sisters in other churches to admire (if not covet) our church facilities? Do we want our denominational leaders to spotlight our buildings and ministries for other churches in the denomination to see? Is it important to us that other churches know the annual increases in our attendance, giving, and baptisms?

This is not to suggest that these accomplishments are wrong. The problem arises when we view ourselves as a significant cause of these accomplishments and when we long for subsequent recognition from others. When we do this, we remove our eyes from the True Source of every good and perfect gift, and we shift our eyes instead to ourselves (Jas. 1:17). And as we shift our eyes to ourselves, we lose sight of the loving priorities of the One who has saved us. When we cease to embrace His priorities, we cease to reflect Him; instead we begin to reflect the nature of the created rather than the Creator.

Neglecting God's priorities in the civil arena is sin. But when we hold up the mirror of our accomplishments, and when our eyes lock onto the image in that mirror, we easily can become enamored by that image and cease to care for the concerns and desires of our loving Father.

Contemporary Idolatry

Do God's people today face the issue of idolatry? Certainly we do not find statues fashioned to represent pagan deities adorning our homes and churches. But we can be tempted to redirect our affections and trust from God and look for other sources of stability and security as well.

Misplaced Affection

As we've discussed, the people of Judah shifted their passion and affections from God and placed them on inanimate objects that reflected their materialism, lust, and pride. We are guilty of the same sin when we focus our passion and affections on objects that reflect our greed, lust, and pride.

For instance, our homes, provisions, automobiles, paychecks, and even our careers can serve as idols if our love has shifted from God and turned to material pleasures. Again, this is not to suggest that having these items is wrong, but when any one of these competes with God for our affections and passions, it has become like an idol. God deserves to be the sole focus of our undivided love.

In the same way, certain items that feed our sensual lusts can have the effect of idols. Sexual lusts can be fed through the Internet, television, videos, books, magazines, and phones.

Our lust for sensual pleasure is not restricted to sexual pleasures. We can direct our affections toward tobacco, alcohol, and drugs.

If we become obsessed with the pleasures of certain hobbies and activities, this, too can be idolatrous. This does not suggest that recreation and hobbies are wrong. When they are viewed properly and exercised in balance, they can be healthy. But when the pleasures from these activities dominate our thinking and become the focus of our longings, we are dangerously like the people of Judah.

In addition, American Christians today wrestle with tangible items that reflect our pride over accomplishments. A car that is purchased to project a certain image of accomplishment; a house that is purchased in a particular neighborhood in order to project a particular status; clothes and jewelry that are designed and worn to announce financial success; each of these can become contemporary equivalents to idols. Whenever we declare our accomplishments through inanimate objects, we reflect the sin of Judah.

Misplaced Trust

For the people of Judah, idolatry not only represented misplaced love but also misplaced trust. They trusted these pagan gods and goddesses for their provisions, stability, and security.

Alas, we face the same temptation today. The Lord promises to care for us and provide for our needs (Matt. 6:25-34; 1 Pet. 5:7). He consistently has shown His love for us and His ability to provide for us; therefore, He deserves our absolute and unwavering trust in matters of provision, stability, and security.

How many of us know this intellectually yet fail to demonstrate practical trust? It is far too easy for us to look to employment, insurance policies, doctors, counselors, retirement plans, and investments as the primary source of provision, stability, and security. While God expects us to be gainfully employed, and while the use of these other resources may be wise under certain circumstances, He still expects us to view Him as the ultimate source of provision and protection. Our jobs don't provide for us; God does! Doctors don't hold our lives in their hands; God does! Our retirement plans and investment portfolios don't secure our future; God does!

God loves us and has promised to take care of us. Furthermore, as a loving Father, He knows how to care for His children. These other areas are made by human hands; when we trust them first for our needs, they are idolatrous equivalents that represent not only our misplaced affections, but also our misdirected trust.

Clearly, our neglect of civil immorality is sin. But it is easy to see why we have shown so little interest in these things that concern God. When His people are caught up in twenty-first century versions of idolatry, we don't care about God's civil concerns. As we focus on the passions that surround our own idols, we lose interest in God's passion.

A Clerical Void?

Some brief points to ponder for religious leaders in the U.S.— the religious leaders of Judah had succumbed to the temptations that plagued Judah—could the same be happening to us today? There is no doubt that ministers face these temptations daily, but have these areas numbed our souls to the urgency of God's passion in the civil arena?

We face the threat of materialism in our ministries. When a larger—or wealthier—church shows interest in our ministry, it's easy to lock onto the financial package involved and "hear God's call" to this new church. When our accommodations aren't up to the standards of our church members, it seems impossible to be content in every circumstance. When finances are tight we may be tempted to reduce the ministries of weddings and funerals to mere financial opportunities. But if God's people are to "seek first His Kingdom," we need to see that example fleshed out in and through our attitudes toward material matters.

We also face sensual temptations. Unlike any other time in history, we are able to turn on a cable channel or computer and sin privately without the church members ever knowing it. In addition to the "private" sexual sins, one recent survey alarmingly revealed that of the pastors who responded about 12 percent admitted to being involved in adultery, and 23 percent had acted in sexually inappropriate ways.[24] As pastors we must heed Paul's admonition to "flee youthful lusts," setting our hearts and minds to guard our purity if we long for God's hand to work through us.

And what about pride? It is so easy for us to focus on the numbers and lose sight of the Master. It's just as easy to focus on the success associated with nice new buildings and then scramble to get new members so that we can pay off the mortgage. Prominent positions within our denominations may be appealing. We long for member and peer approval, but His "well done good and faithful servant" is worth infinitely more than the recognition of any member, fellow pastor, or denominational leader.

Finally, religious leaders also can fall prey to idolatry. We too can redirect our affections from God and place them on tangible, manmade items. We are subject to the lure of "things" that will feed our greed, lust, and pride. Even a new building can be turned from a valuable tool in reaching people for the Lord to an idol that embodies pride in our own accomplishments. Furthermore, church leaders can easily place more confidence in programs, strategies, and emphases than in divine leadership through God's Holy Word.

Our people desperately need to sense God's passion for issues of civil immorality. Our nation's survival depends on it. Even more, our precious Lord desires it. Yet, if this is to become a reality, as pastors we must first set aside these "more pressing issues" in our ministries, and we must each individually embrace His passion.

CONCLUSION

God's children in today's society face the same struggles as His children in ancient Judah faced. As a whole we have failed to embrace and reflect His desires for our civil government. As a result our government is guilty of gross and heinous acts of civil injustices—acts that could have been prevented and acts that could be stopped by our participation in the civil process. But that failure may be a direct result of the diversions that dominate our society. Christians in the U.S. appear to have been derailed by the pursuit of material pleasures, the pursuit of sensual pleasures, pride in our own accomplishments, and the presence of idolatry.

As we have become distracted by these, we have lost sight of the standards that God expects in our civil government, standards that protect His priorities in the areas of justice, relief for the oppressed, and protection for the helpless.

Could it be the reason many of us don't have time to get involved in these civil matters is that we have poured our time and energy into our own individual agendas, agendas that are heavily influenced by the desire for more comfort, more sensual pleasure, and more recognition? Have we lost sight of God's concern in these areas because our eyes are locked on contemporary idols? True, some of us are in situations that require heavy workloads and long hours that may be unrelated to materialism, sensuality, arrogance, and idolatry. But how many of us have become bogged down in one or more of these? How many of us no longer embrace and reflect God's concerns because we are engrossed in our own personal concerns?

We need to be reminded of John's account of God's address to the church in Ephesus. In Revelation 2:4, God told them:

Yet I hold this against you: You have forsaken your first love.

In order for us to address the civil immorality in our nation, we must first repent of these sins and turn our love back to the One who loves us. When we do, we will once again embrace the most pressing issues—priorities of the One who is King over all civil authorities. Perhaps then He will have mercy upon our nation.

1. Also, see Bright, *History of Israel*, 258.

2. Ibid.

3. Bright, 258-259; R. K. Harrison. *Introduction to the Old Testament*, (Grand Rapids: William B. Eerdmans Publishing Company, 1979), 885, 921.

4. F. B. Huey, Jr., "Idolatry," *Zondervan Pictorial Encyclopedia of the Bible*, vol. 3, 242.

5 Cundall, Zondervan Pictorial Encyclopedia of the Bible, vol. 1, 432-433.

6. Richard Swenson, Margin, Nav Press, p. 164.

7. William Branigin, "U.S. Consumer Debt Grows at Alarming Rate," *Washington Post*, January 12, 2004.

8. Ibid.

9. Ibid.

10. "Freedom to Serve," Crown Financial Services, www.cfministry.org/support/freedomtoserve.asp.

11 .Ibid.

12. Ibid.

13. From a conversation with a financial counselor in Central Florida.

14. Crown, Ibid.

15. Conversation, Ibid.

16. Bennett, The Index of Leading Cultural Indicators 2001, 29.

17. U.S. Census Bureau Report, No. 428. State Governments—Summary of Finances: 1990 to 2000, www.census.gov/prod/2003pubs/02statab/stlocgov.pdf.

18. Scott Covington and Curt Swindoll, "Pornography: No Longer a Dirty Little Secret," Crosswalk.com, http://www.crosswalk.com/faith/1224639.html.

19. *Leadership*, Summer 1995, 31-32.

20. Ibid.

21. Ibid.

22. Scott Covington and Curt Swindoll, "Pornography: No Longer a Dirty Little Secret," Crosswalk.com, http://www.crosswalk.com/faith/1224639.html.

23.Ramona Richards, "Dirty Little Secret," Today's Christian Woman, September/October 2003.

24. Terri Lackey, "Catholic Priests Aren't Only Ones Tortured by Sexual Sins," Baptist Press, July 25, 2003.

Chapter 8

WHAT NOW?

Summary and Conclusion

I am a genius!

So thought Tommy Johnson as he strutted through the halls of the Capitol building on his way to the governor's office. The press conference had exceeded even his own high expectations, and the prospects for Gov. Bates's reelection were bright once again. He maintained his trademark cool and controlled image as he approached Bates's office complex, but adrenaline was coursing through his electrified body.

The reporters had bought the story again, just as they had three times before. By the time Johnson finished with them, they believed that Billings's alleged actions were utterly independent of Gov. Bates, and that the good governor could not be held accountable for the independent actions of another person.

But it wasn't the message that convinced the reporters, and it wouldn't be what sold the people when they saw the report on the evening news. No, it wasn't the message, but the *delivery* that made the impact. That's why it was so important to get the news cameras at the press conference.

When Bates recruited him, Johnson was working for a successful marketing firm. He had been so effective for Bates because he brought two essential marketing principles with him to the political arena. He had learned from years of experience that many people make decisions based primarily on emotion rather than factual evidence. The principle had been demonstrated for generations in effective advertising campaigns. When you learn to push the right emotional buttons, many (if not most) people will buy what you are selling, regardless of the facts—which leads to the second marketing principle: Presentation is essentially *everything*.

If your product is presented properly, you will push those emotional buttons—and you *will* sell the product. Even if people don't need the product, even if the product lacks quality, and even if they can't afford it, if the presentation pushes those buttons, people will buy.

Tommy Johnson had learned the secret of marketing Gov. Bates. As he stood before the cameras, he knew which buttons to push. When frenzied reporters who were hungry for a story fired questions at him, he knew how to present his product. Johnson was relaxed and confident without appearing arrogant. He was even a little lighthearted, joking a bit with some of the reporters. His mannerisms gave the impression that everything was OK and that there was no cause for alarm (if you appear uncomfortable or uneasy for any reason, the customer will be suspicious and might not buy your product).

When the reporters pushed the issue of Bates's repeated problems with his appointees, Johnson turned it around and presented Bates as an honest servant who had been continually harassed and victimized by partisan politics and by certain members of the press who were probably more concerned about advancing a journalistic career than with reporting the facts. Johnson knew that people like to side with the victim, and he used this to his advantage.

Tommy Johnson had become a master of marketing his product, Gov. P.J. Bates. He knew that most of the people would vote in the next election based on their emotions rather than on the facts. So Johnson played to the emotions—and he played very well. His presentation had become virtually flawless, and the people seemed to be buying.

These thoughts raced through his mind as he approached the office door. Perhaps his performance today would lead Bates to appoint him as the campaign manager for his reelection bid. Johnson had served Bates well, and he obviously could turn lemons into lemonade. Maybe today's press conference would "seal the deal." If so, there was an even brighter future facing him, for everyone knew Bates had his sights on a seat in the U.S. Senate and maybe even the presidency. Johnson saw himself as a tremendous asset to Bates and was sure Bates recognized that benefit as well.

Johnson walked up to Liz Thompson's desk. "Hi, Liz," he offered.

"Hi, Tommy," she replied through her warm smile. "We watched the conference on the monitor. You did a fine job, as usual."

"Thanks," he responded. "Is Governor Bates able to see me?"

"He's expecting you," Liz answered. "Go on in."

Tommy Johnson felt his heart start to pound as he reached for the door. He stopped, instantly made a mental adjustment, stood a little straighter, and remarked to himself, "Remember, Johnson, presentation is everything."

What will be the outcome of future elections? Will the various candidates on the local, state, and national levels be elected because of marketing strategies or because of their qualifications and their stand on the issues? There is no doubt that the assorted campaign managers across this nation are fine-tuning each candidate's image and planning powerful campaign commercials to sway public opinion. But will our city, county, state, and national leaders be chosen primarily because of slick political packaging or because of their qualifications, stance, and character?

The answer to this question may rest in the hands of God's children. If we will respond to God's Word and share His passion for civil justice in our land, the outcome could be bright for the people of our land. On the other hand, if we fail to embrace and reflect His desire and concerns in this area, the prospects are indeed grim. But just how far does God expect us to go with our civil responsibilities? What exactly does He expect of us in this coming election? As one person asked, "If failure in my civil responsibilities hinders my worship, what must I do to be sure that God hears my prayers?"

We'd like to answer the question by considering some specific applications that correspond to the principles discussed in the book. Then we will attempt to eliminate some potential misconceptions that might arise from these principles.

WHAT IT MEANS FOR US

If we truly long to embrace His passion for justice, and if we sincerely wish to reflect an accurate image of God to the watching world, what tangible steps should we take?

We do not propose to submit an exhaustive, legalistic list to serve as some sort of spiritual litmus test, or to be used as the final and ultimate standard for biblical compliance. In fact, if someone has become alarmed enough to sincerely ask such a question, that person probably already is headed down the right path. Here are suggestions to help guide God's children on that road.

Pray

First and foremost, serious prayer is called for in at least four areas.

A. Our most obvious prayer need is that of confessing our sins to God. All of us are guilty of offending God's standards of justice in one way or another (Rom. 3:23). Often we have been silent in the face of injustice suffered by others. We may need to confess the sins of greed, lust, pride, or idolatry. We may need to confess our failure to serve as "salt" and "light" in civil society. Confessing our sins may seem a bitter cup to drink, but it is crucial for our relationship with God. Swallowing our pride is the first step toward humility and repentance (1 John 1:9). Joy comes, however, in knowing that God promises to forgive our sins and that He actually *delights* to show mercy (Mic. 7:18).

B. Having confessed our own sin, the next logical step is to pray for our government. First Timothy 2:1-4 exhorts us to pray for our government officials so that we may experience peace and tranquility as a society and live our lives in godliness and dignity. The turbulence and discord that we experience in our society may well be the direct result of our failure to follow the biblical exhortation to pray for our leaders.

C. A third key area of prayer involves the need to ask for individual wisdom and discernment while considering the various candidates. James 1:5 promises that those who ask God for wisdom will receive it. And we need it—especially when it comes to the process of selecting those who will lead us. As the opening illustration of this chapter points out, campaigns are designed to push people's emotional buttons and gain their votes. Sometimes it is difficult to see past the facade to get a genuine picture of the candidate—that's why we need to pray.

Our loving Father can be trusted to safely navigate us through thick fog. He will direct us if we will look to Him for guidance.

D. Finally, we all need to pray intently for the outcome of the next election and the elections to follow. We are in a defining time for our nation, and the results of the impending elections will significantly determine our nation's future, especially in the area of civil justice. We need to be praying for the Lord to raise up those who will stand for His priorities in the civil arena.

Become Informed

Having prayed, the next logical step for us is to do some very basic individual research on the candidates, whether on the local, state, or national level. To be able to vote intelligently, we need to know some crucial information about each of the candidates.

A. We need to know where the candidates stand on issues that bear on God's principles of justice. What are the candidates' positions on abortion, infanticide, and assisted suicide? Where do they stand on "gay rights," same sex "marriage" and civil unions, and sensitivity training in our public schools that promotes "alternate lifestyles?" What are their positions on campaign reform, tort reform, welfare reform, and corrections reform? How do they view state-run gambling?

If these views are not presented in the local newspaper or in campaign literature, a call or an e-mail to the local campaign headquarters inquiring about the candidate's position should be able to produce these details. It's well worth the time it takes to get an official, on-the-record response.

B. In addition to a candidate's official stance on the issues, it helps to know of the candidate's activities in these areas. If a candidate has held public office before, find out how he voted in the areas under consideration. What policies has she supported that relate to issues of justice? Many organizations produce voters' guides that set forth the voting records or policy positions of candidates on a range of issues. If the candidate has been in a position to make appointments, find out how his appointees performed with respect to the issues under discussion. Have the appointees advanced civil justice or attempted to stifle it? Have they supported government-sanctioned sexual promiscuity or opposed it? Have their activities consistently embraced the sanctity of human life or mocked it? An appointee's actions sometimes reveal more about the candidate than their official platform.

C. Find out if the candidate has openly courted special interest groups that stand on either side of the moral issues. Has the candidate sought and received heavy campaign financing from various groups? Remember, it's difficult for candidates to remain unbiased when certain groups have helped underwrite their campaigns. In the same vein, has the candidate received gifts and "perks" from various lobbyists? If so, what kind and how much? Again, a call to the candidate's local headquarters can provide this information. And if the members of the campaign staff are hesitant to provide the details, call their opponent's office. The opposition will be more than happy to provide this information.

D. After researching a candidate's position on issues, take note of the candidate's personal pattern in the areas we've discussed. A candidate's personal lifestyle may be a good indicator of how the candidate will approach moral issues in government. Don't expect perfection. Everyone has sinned, and we will never have perfect officials in office. But if a person's private life is characterized by ongoing and obvious instances of immorality, Christians should question whether that person is able to represent their convictions. If a candidate has a history of sexual infidelity or immorality, is it likely that candidate will value the sanctity of marriage and family in the public arena? If a candidate is known for business practices that have victimized others, is it likely that candidate will be sensitive to the needs of the helpless? If a candidate has demonstrated a history of breaking promises or of being deceptive, is it likely that person can be trusted to keep campaign promises?

Granted, it may take a little time to research a candidate's official stand, official record, and personal behavior and then compare them to the standards God has set for government. But if it matters to the Lord, shouldn't it matter to us? If it takes a few hours to gather this information, isn't that a sound investment for those who embrace God's concerns and wish to reflect Him to the world?

After prayer and research, get involved in the process. Having prayerfully decided on the candidate who will best stand for God's standards for civil justice, one does well to educate others and to support or oppose various candidates. Christians should not avoid political involvement out of some misguided sense of piety. Edmund Burke rightly observed, "The only thing necessary for the triumph of evil is for good men to do nothing."[1] Nature abhors a vacuum. If Christians fail to participate in the political arena, it will be occupied by others.

Vote

Finally, Christians must exercise their right to vote. This may seem painfully obvious, but the sad reality is that most Christians stay home on voting day. As we've pointed out, more than half of the people who attend church don't vote. Our ongoing failure to meet our civic and biblical responsibilities has cost the nation dearly.

After voting, we need to continue to monitor the way in which government addresses issues relating to God's principles of justice so that they can inform elected officials of their concerns and desires. On a national level this can be difficult, but a number of resources are available. In the Appendix of this book, we have listed a number of organizations that provide helpful information for use in keeping abreast of the issues. These same organizations often provide contact information for our elected officials.

What we have outlined is not intended to serve as an exhaustive list of the responsibilities for proper Christian citizenship. It is crucial that we all pray, investigate the candidates, vote prayerfully and responsibly, and follow up with the elected officials. And having prayed about it, some also may feel led to financially support a candidate's campaign. Others may feel led to run for a particular office. God may prompt some to start an "Issues Awareness Team" in their church to inform the congregation of key civil activities. Still others may be inclined to start prayer meetings in their church for our nation and her leaders. When God's people have open hearts, He is able to lead them in the ways that will best accomplish His purposes.

Again, the activities we recommend may take some time out of your busy schedule, but if the Lord is concerned about the way our government dispenses justice, shouldn't Christians embrace that concern as well? There is a strong likelihood that the involvement of Christians in the civil arena will change the course of our nation and her future. Even if things do not change, the people of God can rest in the knowledge that they have shared God's concerns and carried out their civic responsibility. Regardless of the outcome of our efforts, Christians are called to engagement and to project God's love and nature to the watching world.

WHAT THIS STUDY DOES NOT MEAN FOR US

This type of study may give rise to potential misconceptions and misguided conclusions. To avoid the prospect of misdirected emotion and energy, let's remove all doubt in several areas.

First, this study in no way suggests that our call to civic engagement is a higher priority than our call to proclaim the glorious truth of the gospel. God's primary concern for humanity is redemption through the atoning sacrifice of His Son Jesus Christ, not political utopia. Jesus died to save us from our sin, not from political and civil collapse. Our highest priority is to be living and verbal witnesses of God's saving grace in a dying world. As one theologian observed, "The dead are not raised by politics." But to embrace the priority of proclaiming the gospel does not relieve us of our civic duty. God expects us to obey Him in both regards.

A second misconception could be that spiritual revival will come to our nation through our civil leaders. While this may have happened in the Old Testament account of Jonah, there is no indication that a "trickle down" effect will necessarily be applied to our nation. At the same time, if we refuse to embrace and reflect God's concerns in the area of government, we have no reason to expect national revival to sweep our land.

The next misconception that we want to avoid is that this study calls for (or supports) the notion of a Christian or religious "takeover" of the government. Our nation was not established as a theocracy. Our government was not established as a religious institution in the manner of ancient Israel and Judah. This study does not suggest that our government must become "Christian," in the sense that all of our leaders and all government policy must be directly tied to a religious structure or institution. We are not advocating what some have called "reconstructionism." Similarly, this study does not advocate the notion of a "Christian" political party. Some Christian organizations do an excellent job of informing Christians of key issues and of motivating them to action, but that role is vastly different from being an organized political party.

An additional concern relates to the potential for a legalistic and harsh application of the principles in this study. The United States does not need an "All Saints Gestapo" to police Christians across the nation and intimidate them into acceptance of a prescribed and pre-approved agenda. Each Christian should pray individually and personally seek to find the candidates whom he or she believes will best stand for God's standards. Each person must ultimately answer to God—not to a church, not to a pastor, and not to a Christian special interest group—for his or her vote. This is not to say that pastors should not address God's standards of justice from the pulpit or identify candidates who have *clearly* violated those standards. We believe they should. But, in our view, no pastor, church, or religious group has the right to bind the conscience of an individual or to dictate one's vote.

Finally, this study is not intended to justify or support any form of bullying or intimidation of our leaders as they relate to the issues under discussion. The apostle Paul reminds us that part of the "fruit of the Spirit" is *gentleness* (Gal. 5:23). When Jesus entered Jerusalem just before His betrayal and crucifixion, He came as a *gentle* King (Matt. 21:5). God calls His children to speak the truth, but to speak it in love (Eph. 4:15). He also calls His children to show honor and respect to civil leaders (1 Pet. 2:17). It is possible for us to call our leaders to compliance with God's civil standards without resorting to words or actions that undercut our witness.

What will happen in coming elections? Will the likes of Tommy Johnson have their way with the American public? Will the nation be duped by slick political marketing strategies? The answer may rest in the hands of God's people in the United States of America. If we will pray, become informed, vote, and follow up with elected officials, the results may be spectacular.

Perhaps the more critical question is, "Will God's people in America recognize His passion for justice and choose to reflect that passion at the polls?" If we will turn from our sinful preoccupations and embrace God's priorities for our government, if we will lovingly reflect those priorities in the civil arena, if we will repent of our sinful silence, we may well experience the blessing of watching God turn our nation back from a path that leads to destruction. If we don't, we may well behold God's heavy hand of judgment crashing down upon our nation in ways we have never imagined before. If this happens because of the sinful silence of Christians in the civil arena, the Christian community will face the prospect of experiencing that national judgment along with the rest of the nation. The nation's future may, indeed, rest in the hands of God's people.

It most certainly rests in the hands of God.

---

1. WorldofQuotes.Com, Historic Quotes and Proverbs Archives, www.world-ofquotes.com/author/Edmund-Burke/1/.

Appendix
Organizational Resources for
Engaging the Civil Process

The Center for Reclaiming America, D. James Kennedy, president—
www.reclaimamerica.org
- Provides training, and support "to all those interested in positively affecting the culture and renewing the vision of our Founding Fathers."
- Provides special resources for pastors and churches

Concerned Women For America, Beverly LaHaye, founder—
www.cwfa.org
- Daily radio broadcast
- Publications and alerts

Eagle Forum, Phyllis Schlafley, president—www.eagleforum.org
- Publications and alerts
- Provides "Scoreboard" on key congressional votes

Family Research Council, Tony Perkins, president—www.frc.org
- Daily email update
- Publications and alerts
- Witherspoon Fellowship
- "Score Card" on key congressional votes

Focus on the Family, James Dobson, president—www.family.org
- Daily Radio Broadcast—frequently addresses issues and welcomes guests who speak on key issues
- *Citizen* Magazine
- Citizen Link email—provides daily articles and updates on key issues

For Faith and Family, Richard Land, president—SBC Ethics and
Religious Liberty Commission—www.erlc.com
- Daily Radio Broadcast—frequently addresses issues and welcomes guests who speak on key issues
- *For Faith and Family* Magazine
- IvoteValues.com—A nation-wide voter registration and information emphasis and tour

Prison Fellowship, Charles Colson, president—www.pfm.org
- Breakpoint Radio Broadcast
- Breakpoint email
- Wilberforce Forum
- Justice Fellowship

With Gratitude

A work of substance is rarely accomplished by one or two people, but rather by a team of people committed to the same goal. This book would never have become reality if it were not for the people God brought into our lives, going back ten years when this project began, and even beyond.

Ken would like to thank:
- My wife, Amy, whose selfless sacrifices have enabled me to serve as an activist in the causes we both hold dear;
- My parents, Kay and Fay Connor, the best role models a son could have;
- Martha Sims, Jan Early, and Camille Godwin, friends and colleagues who have supported me in all of my professional endeavors.

John would like to thank:
- Debbie—my bride, my sweetheart, my dearest and deepest friend—who has put up with so much from me for 25 years, always supporting, encouraging, and loving me;
- My parents, Cliff and Sue Revell, who instilled in me a love for God and His Word;
- My colleagues—my dear friends at the SBC Executive Committee who have stood by me as I labored through the process;
- My brothers and sisters at Long Hollow Baptist Church, many of whom helped pray this project into reality;
- My Old Testament seminary professor, Robert Hubbard, who reminded his students that 2 Timothy 3:16 applies as much to the Old Testament as the New Testament;
- Bill Merrell, my boss, my writing coach, my brother, and my dear friend.

Together we would like to thank:
- George Poulos, for introducing Ken and John, and who challenged John to biblically evaluate our civil responsibilities as Christians—which led to this study;
- Fred Revell, who originally came up with the idea for the two of us to write this book;

(*continued*)

- Dr. D. James Kennedy and Dr. R.C. Sproul, who read early chapters and offered strong encouragement and rich counsel;
- The countless family members and dear friends who have labored through early manuscripts, offering wise counsel;
- Our editorial, design, and typesetting team—Karen Cole, Carolyn Gregory, Andy Beachum, and Leanne Adams. You all helped make this dream come true;
- Rachel McRae and Chris Rodgers at LifeWay, Larry Carpenter at FaithWorks, and Karl Huddleston at RR Donnelley—thank you for seeing the Lord's hand in this and for believing in us enough to give us a shot.

And most importantly, our Heavenly Father, *who is able to do far more abundantly beyond all that we ask or think, according to the power that works within us, to Him be the glory in the church and in Christ Jesus to all generations forever and ever. Amen.*

About Ginosko Publishing

"Ginosko" (ği-nōs-kō) is the Greek verb for "knowing." The concept embodied in the word extends beyond mere intellectual knowledge to include intimate and experiential knowledge.

Ken Connor and John Revell have established and embraced the following life goal:

> "To know and love God and His Word as much as possible,
> and to help as many as possible do the same."

Ginosko Publishing flows out of that goal. The logo is the Greek letter "Gamma," the first letter in Ginosko, over an open Bible. The products developed and released by Ginosko Publishing will have the express purpose of drawing people into a deeper understanding and appreciation of God's Word, and thereby a closer relationship with Him.

Now this is eternal life: that they may **know** *you,*
the only true God, and Jesus Christ, whom you have sent.
(John 17:3)

For more information and resources, go to:
www.ToKnowGod.org.

About the Authors

Ken Connor is a civil trial attorney in the Washington, D.C. area. He has most recently served as president of the Family Research Council and as the National Chairman of Care Net, a network of crisis pregnancy centers sponsored by the Christian Action Council. His activities have been featured on *ABC's Prime Time Live*, the *MacNeil Lehrer News Hour*, and *CBS, ABC, NBC, FOX*, and *CNN News*. He has also been a frequesnt guest on the *Focus on the Family* radio broadcast, and he has written editorials for numerous newspapers, including *USA TODAY, The Washington Post, The Atlanta Journal-Constitution*, and *The Washington Times*. Recently Florida Governor Jeb Bush appointed Ken as lead attorney defending "Terri's Law," in the Terri Schiavo litigation.

John Revell has been Associate Editor of *SBC LIFE*, the official journal of the Southern Baptist Convention Executive Committee, since 1996. Prior to that he served in pastoral ministry for ten years in Long Island, N.Y., and in South Florida. His articles have been printed, reprinted, and cited in numerous publications, and he has been quoted in such publications as *Newsweek, The Los Angeles Times*, and *The Boston Globe*.